Proverbs 31:10

For you p. 106

THE EDGE OF HIS GARMENT

To Judy,
May the writings in this book bless you and bring you closer to God.
May God continue to bless you as you seek Him out in your life.
God loves you.
God bless!
Marietta G.

THE EDGE OF HIS GARMENT

INSPIRING MEDITATIONS AND PRAYERS CONCERNING LIFE'S MEANING

MARIBETH NORMAN

WinePress Publishing (PO Box 428, Enumclaw, WA 98022) functions only as book publisher. As such, the ultimate design, content, editorial accuracy, and views expressed or implied in this work are those of the author.

ISBN 13: 978-1-4141-1649-5
ISBN 10: 1-4141-1649-7
Library of Congress Catalog Card Number: 2009911636

Touch

and

Believe

DEDICATION

I dedicate this book to Jesus Christ, My Lord and Savior, without whom I would be nothing.

My children, Terry and Justin, the loves of my life here on earth. I love you both. My new granddaughter, Khloé Ann. I love you.

My sister, Nancy, and her husband, Joe Gordon. Thank you for your artwork ideas for the book. I love you both. My sister—Patty Smith—thank you for always being there for me. I love you. My brothers Johnny and Robbie. Thanks for the brotherly support. Thanks to all of you for the love of our family. I love you all. I hope now you understand my journey as a child.

My best friend, Rita Fletcher, who is like a sister and always there for me. I love you. My spiritual advisors and friends, Minister Carolyn Napier and Elder Jo Ann Betton. Thank you both for all the advice and support you offered while working with me and the book. I love you both. Mrs. Williams, thank you for your love throughout the years.

My spiritual friend Larry Ballew, the man God sent into my life to teach me how to listen again to the Lord. A special thank you, Larry. I will be so grateful to you forever. May God continue to bless you, Deanie, and the family; and to Jewel, thank you for your love and letting me in the circle.

In memory of Ike and Gail Coleman, two strong people who taught me about family and commitments. I love and miss you both.

In memory of my mother, Mary Elizabeth Norman, a remarkable woman who introduced me to God and taught me how to have a relationship with Him. Mom, I am grateful that God gave me the opportunity to read you this dedication before you went home to Him. You told me in the hospital you didn't believe that you had a deep impact on my life with God; but as I shared with you, yes mom, you certainly did. Thank you mom for everything. I love and miss you.

CONTENTS

PRAISE

GRACE

ACKNOWLEDGMENTS

I would like to acknowledge some people who in their special ways supported this book. They all played a part in God's plan to have me finish this book.

Deacon Pete Labita, of Christ the King Church, thanks for the great Bible lessons. They were God's plan. Pastor Keene, thanks for your God-given words of wisdom on my visits to Kingdom Christian Center Church. Bishop Harold Ray and Pastor Brenda Ray, of Redemptive Life Fellowship Church, thanks for your kindness and prayers of support.

Janelle Sparks, one of my spiritual editors, thanks for all your hard work on the book. Skylar Burris, another editor, thank you. Richard and Toyia Belle, thank you for the spiritual conversations and support. Kate Wiley, thanks for listening to God and giving me the opportunity in Florida; that action led me to finish the book. Glenn Guice, thanks for your support and connecting me with Tim Luke. His advice guided me to publish the book.

Jabez L.I.F.T. Ministry friends and sisters, Rita, Carolyn, Jo Ann, Virginia, Ruby, Pam, Donna, Verna, Losie, LaTonya, Annette (Freda), Tonya, Sandy, Shirleen, Fredda, Beverly, Terri M., Sherri, Terri H., Gail, Diane, Rose, Ernestine, Ann, Janet, Sheila, Marla, Georgia, Charlotte, Laren, and Carol. Your encouragement and prayers meant more to me than you will ever know. Thank you and I love you all.

Thanks to all who helped me by praying for me during this journey. If I failed to thank anyone, charge it to my head and not my heart.

PREFACE

One cold, early November morning in 2003, as I was sleeping so comfortably with my covers around me, I heard a voice. It was not an audible voice, but a voice so strong that I will remember it for the rest of my life. I heard the voice say, "Blessed are those who will minister for Him and serve just One."

I immediately sat up in my bed. Somewhat shaken, I asked, "What?" No one was in the bedroom except me, but I heard the voice repeat the same words. I again asked, "What?"

Then the voice said, "Write it down." I knew it was God, but that knowledge didn't diminish my nervousness. So I wrote the words down on some paper beside my bed. Then as more and more words continued to come, I wrote them down. That was the beginning of several writings, which led to *The Edge of His Garment.*

The Edge of His Garment consists of a collection of powerful writings telling us that God is still there for us to touch and talk with. You will find the writings inspiring, comforting, reassuring, mercy filled, grace giving, praiseworthy, and a powerful expression of God's love for you. They will transform your life, as you know it now, into something that only you and God will understand.

These writings are meditations conveying messages from God, and for each person they will hold a different meaning. These meditations will help you experience God's love when you feel unloved or in need of love, God's comfort in your times of sorrow or grieving, God's joy when you need happiness, the inspiration of God when you are depressed or need uplifted, and the things God wants to tell you. Mainly the book will remind you that He loves you.

Like the woman in the Bible with the issue of blood who knew that all she needed to do was touch Jesus' garment and be healed, so too will you feel the power of God as you read the writings in *The Edge of His Garment.* You will be extending your hand to touch the Lord. The woman knew she was beyond the point of any earthly healing for her issue of blood. She believed, and by her faith Jesus healed her.

Isn't that how we feel at times in our day-to-day life? That our problems are beyond anything or anyone on earth that can help us, and we just need to talk with Him? Sometimes when you find yourself desperately needing to talk with someone or picking up the telephone only to receive a voice recording from the other end, pick up this book instead and talk with Him. Seek beyond your boundaries and touch the spiritual edge. Read the writings. Don't be afraid. Only believe and you will be speaking with the Lord. You will find the One you have been seeking. You will feel the powerful touch of the Lord upon your heart. You will be touching God.

God healed the woman of her blood issue because of her faith. You too will experience that same relief from your problems and concerns. She found her peace and you will find yours. As you read these writings, by your faith, He will answer you. Even if you are questioning your faith, you will be changed after reading *The Edge of His Garment*.

I thought these meditations and prayers would only be for family members and friends, but God led me down a very different path with this book. The book is meant to serve as a resource for people, now and in future generations, when they need to touch the Lord. At the end of each section, a personal reflection note page has been included for your study and spiritual growth.

When I wrote these writings, God sometimes gave me the words; sometimes the words arose after conversations with Him, and sometimes God just spoke to me. I was not trying to put words into God's mouth, but I wrote as understanding was given to me. You will understand as you read the book. The writings in this book are for all of God's children, even those who do not believe.

As you read this book, remember that it is God who is talking to you, and all you have to do is listen. Now read and touch the edge of His garment, and feel God's glory, power, grace, and love as it flows from Him to you.

The healing touch of His garment rests in your belief in Him. Touch and believe!

INSPIRATION

Jesus said, "Someone touched me;
I know that power has gone out from me."

—Luke 8:46 (NIV)

JUST ONE TOUCH

Just one touch of the Master's hand upon my soul
has changed my life forever.
The touch upon my ears has let me hear His voice.
The touch upon my eyes has let me see His vision.
The touch upon my tongue has let me speak His Word
to others and with others.

The touch upon my heart has made me love others
as I thought I never could; He has let me feel
and give His love to others.
The touch upon my hands
has made me want to help others in need of Him.

Your touch upon my mind has made me understand
Your ways, Lord,
but no understanding is needed:
one just needs to believe.
Your touch upon my soul
has given me the strength of the Holy Spirit.

Just that one touch, Lord, and You have changed me;
my life has never been the same.
The touch brought me closer to the Lord,
closer than I ever thought I could be,
but now I understand with just one touch.

Extensions of His touch and love were given to me
with just one touch,
a touch I am so thankful to have received.

Just one touch, one touch from the Lord,
and I am in Him.

Seek first the Kingdom of Heaven and all Shall be added.

AN OBEDIENT CHILD

What is an obedient child of God?

A child who listens to the Word of God.
A child who knows what to do and when to do it.
A child who follows what is commanded of him.
A child who shares her laughter with the souls of others.
A child who stands before God and asks for blessings to
come his way and to the way of others.
A child who stands before God without sin.
A child who asks God to forgive others for their split tongues.
A child who does not throw stones at others.
A child who sees the good in all people.
A child who holds the hand of man through the good
and bad storms.
A child who brings in the sheaves of wheat to feed on the
Word of God from the earth in which God sowed them.
A child who thirsts for the water that God gives to all.
A child who thinks of others first.
A child who touches the sick and the hand of death among them.
A child who sees the ways of God and lets the angels lead
her along the ways.
A child who is still in mind, but loving in his heart toward others.
A child who hears the cries of the people and speaks to God for
their tears.
A child who puts aside her fear…for an obedient child knows no
fear of the Lord…for she is pure at heart.

Who is an obedient child of God?
You are My one…you are.

MY CONVERSATION WITH GOD

How do I tell people that God is talking to me,
when they will not listen?
How can I get them to understand?
What can I say differently to make their ears turn toward me?
What can I tell them that they feel they don't already know?
What experience can I describe, without them feeling
they have already done this before?

Tell me, God, how can I convey Your message?
How, Lord, how can I tell others about the way
they are to follow?
How, Lord, can I talk with people and get them to listen
when they will not choose to do so?
How, Lord? Please show me the way.
Show me the path to go and tell me the words to say.
How, Lord, can I get Your people to listen?
How can I tell people God is talking to me
when they will not listen?
How, Lord, how?

(His Response)

I say unto you, you will know the way and the Word to speak to others. As you speak, they will know it is Me speaking through you. As you speak, they will listen. As you go, they will follow. As you tell, they will want to hear more—more of the ways and times of Christ when I was present on earth and now present in your life. As you tell, they will follow and obey. Just speak, child, speak, and they will hear.
It is Me speaking through you. It is Me they will hear.
It is Me talking to them; they will come. They will come.
Just obey and talk with Me; they will follow and obey.

SUPPORT OF THE LORD

Times in your life when you think I am not listening.
Times when you think I have not heard your calls.
Times when you think you are alone.
Times in your life when you think I am not there.
These times and others are all your imagination.

I am with you always. I love you and have been with you
through all the days of your life.
I have been with you through all your calls for help.
I have heard you calling My name at night,
when you thought no one was listening.

I am here. I am the support that gets you up each day.
The support that helps you speak to Me and others.
The support to hear My name as you call it from your lips.
Your support through the tears and all your hidden fears; they are not
hidden from Me, My child.

I am your light in any darkness.
I see your fears and take them from you to provide
you comfort when you need it.

SUPPORT OF THE LORD

I am your comfort, as I have always been,
ever since you were a child, when I placed you on earth.
I will not leave you. I am your rock, comfort, and support.
When you need to call on Me, say,
"Lord, please give me Your support."
My child, when you say these words you will know
I am with you.
I will hear, listen, and lighten your burdens.

Just as I called on My Father,
so too may you call on Me,
I will listen and provide you My support.
I will answer your call.

THE SHIELD

You are created in My image.
You are beautiful, so masterfully made as My work.
How can I not love you? How can I turn you away?

I want you beside Me always.
I do not want you to feel pain.
I do not want you to go through life without knowing
the feeling of My love.
I gave you the warmth of My love;
feel it by loving others.
Help others who are lost
to experience the feeling I have given you,
so it too may comfort them.

I gave you free will, and
I want what you want in this life.
You cannot work outside of My plan for you.
Give all of yourself to Me.
Let Me take your struggles and burdens.
Just ask, My child—just ask.

I will protect you all the days of your life.
Have faith and believe in Your Lord.
Faith is your shield against all evil.
No harm will overcome you
if you have your shield of faith.
Your shield will be in front of you,
and I will always be beside you.

THE SHIELD

Remember: declaring that no evil exists is the biggest evil.
The shield of your faith will guide you past your fears.
You are blessed and created in My image.
I will not let you go unprotected.
I will not let thee go.
I will not let your shield go down.

Stay close in the protection of your Lord
with your shield of faith.
Believe.

WRAP YOUR ARMS AROUND GOD

Wrap your arms around God when you feel lonely.
Wrap your arms around God when you feel you need a hug
or comfort for your soul.
Know that God's love is always there for you.
Know that God loves you in all His many ways.

Wrap your arms around God and talk with Him when you need
someone to listen.
He will answer you and listen to your thoughts.
He is there;
He is always there for you.

You will come to have a beautiful relationship with God.
He will become your best friend,
your true spiritual companion.
He will talk with you and provide you the feeling of His love.
You will know the feeling of the Trinity:
The Holy Spirit, Jesus Christ, and the Lord thy God as One.

Wrap your arms around God
and take hold of what He has to give you.
Wrap your arms around God and offer all of yourself to Him.
You will never be alone. You will never be afraid.

WRAP YOUR ARMS AROUND GOD

In times of loneliness and fear say,
"Lord be with me." You will hear Him answer,
"I am always with you. How can you be lonely or afraid?
You cannot."

Just talk with the Lord and come to know Him.
He is waiting for you to speak and seek Him
in your times of trouble.
Seek Him in your heart.

Wrap your arms around God. He is listening always.
Wrap your arms around God. He is the first love of your life and
forever your comfort.
Wrap your arms around God; this is a golden opportunity to have a
relationship with Him in your life.
Do not let this time pass away,
for if it does, you have been led astray.

THE PORTAL

Enter the Kingdom of God through the door.
The door is open to all, but to enter you must be prepared.

Give up worldly riches and the goods of the earth.
Give up yourself to Me.
Give up your fears to Me and know the place of My love.
Give up your negative sayings and ways.
Give up your evil thoughts; you cannot enter without a mind of clean thoughts of others and your Lord.

Walk in My footsteps to the door.
Enter only when you are truly prepared.
The door is the portal to My house,
your resting place forever with Me.
It is the portal to My love
and your everlasting life in Me, Jesus Christ.
It is the portal to the love of My Father.
Enter only when you are truly prepared.

When you walk through the door,
all the riches of the world will be bestowed on you.
The blessings will flow from Me and out through you.
The words will utter freely from you,
like sounds of music flowing on the ears of angels on earth.
All your needs will be supplied.
Everything you have given up on earth to enter the kingdom,
I will give back to you threefold.

THE PORTAL

It is easier for one who is prepared to enter through the door
than it is for one
who cannot give up riches and earthly ways.

The door is the opening, the portal to My kingdom.
Come walk through and know the riches
I have waiting for you.

A PEARL IN THE PALM OF GOD'S HAND

Your life is like the pearls of the sea:
rich and deeply buried,
but revealing a treasure upon discovery.

The pearl is formed over time,
starting with a speck,
as is man's life with a speck of dust,
but a speck developed into the image of Me,
which I projected so I might know Myself in you
and the likeness of Me.

A pearl requires time to mold and shape itself,
to become a thing of beauty;
so too man's life forms from birth through years and times.
From times of being taught about Me, My Word, and ways,
from times of learning and grasping My teachings.

All of these things form the man in My likeness
through the years, until one day,
his life is formed as a beautiful life of Christ:
molded and shaped through time
like the beauty of a discovered pearl.
How similar the two are to Me in their formation;
the pearl and your life.

I hold your life like a pearl in the palm of My hand:
so beautifully formed and yet an undiscovered treasure
waiting for My finding.

Live your life like I want, and I will hold you close always,
like a treasured pearl in the palm of My hand.

LETTERS OF CHRIST

You are a letter of Christ written on the hearts
of those you have touched.

The letter is not written in ink,
but with a spiritual embellishment,
fulfilling others with Christ formed in them.

You are to proclaim the news
that the day of Christ is now at hand.
You will instill within hearts
God's love, and they will know they are His people.

The letter is forceful and telling, but mild and gentle
in its delivery of His message.

Fulfill your duty as a letter.
Tell of the Word, of the Truth, and the message of the Lord.

The letter is not written in stone, not written on parchment,
but on the fleshly hearts of those it touches.
The letter is set as a seal on God's heart.
The letter will go and follow the way the Lord intends.

(God Speaking)

For wherever it goes, I go,
whomever it follows, I follow.
I am as indelible ink upon your heart.
I am with you always,
always with you, as the letter in your spiritual form.
Read and know of the spiritual writings in the letter,
and you will know Me.

SWEETER THAN HONEY

Speak not against your neighbor or friend;
hold your tongue about you.
Speak only with the thought of your Lord
on your lips.
It is a truehearted person who waits
and speaks only the good.

For to whisper and taunt is displeasing to Me.
One who whispers divides the house of the Lord,
and that is not what I want.

The words of the wise are sent from Me;
commit yourself and your tongue to your Lord.
I will control the thoughts and words
that come your way.

The words of the whisperer are damaging to the soul.
The more the words are spoken,
the more you separate yourself from My kingdom.

Do you want to go alone?
Do you want to speak wrongly of your neighbor?
Your neighbor is also a child of Mine.
If you speak against your neighbor,
you also speak against Me.

SWEETER THAN HONEY

Words can be sweeter than honey
or sour as vinegar.
Let your words be true.
Let them come from a heart that is meek and lowly,
full of love for Me and My people.

Let your words be as sweet music to My ears.
Let My spirit talk, and you will listen.
You will be a mouthpiece for your Lord,
speaking only the truth and love of your Lord.

A whisperer is a separator of everlasting life
and death to My kingdom.
Do not let your words be the death of you.
Let your words be kind and pleasing,
your lips forever in service of My spirit.

Do not be a whisperer of ill faith against your neighbor
and your Lord.
Do not stray from My fold.
Be a wise one who spreads My Word from your heart.
Let your words be as a honeycomb,
sweet to Me and pleasing to the soul.

BREATH OF LIFE

I blew into you the breath of My life.
The breath that lets you speak to others through Me,
to speak as I spoke to others, and to know My language and love.

I gave you life,
to walk the earth and know the beauties of the earth.
The sun and creatures of the earth I have made for you.

I gave you the body, mind, and soul.
When the body, mind, and soul come together in unity,
then I AM made flesh.
Flesh as a son of man.
Flesh like that made in the image of Me.
Flesh into which I blew the spirit so that man could live.

The breath was given so man would know himself in the highest
version of the spirit bestowed upon him.
The breath was given so man would know his soul
and his soul's experience in the highest form,
through the unity of the body and the mind.

As you breathe the breath of life, you will know the unity,
truth, and Word of Me.
Your breath of life and your spirit will be open to your Lord,
revealing all your thoughts and feelings.

BREATH OF LIFE

Prepare your breath of life by hearing your soul.
Listen to the Holy Spirit and allow Him unity in you.
The Spirit cannot enter unless you call,
and your breath cannot be complete without Him.

I breathed into you the breath of My life.
Feel the breath of My Spirit;
let it fulfill your soul. Then become complete in Me.

BREATHE AGAIN

I was dead with no life or breath.
I was living in a human flesh with no spirit,
but I have been reborn.

God brought me out of death.
God gave me a new breath, the breath of the Holy Spirit.
I had a death to God,
but God has risen me from that death.
He has let me see and feel the splendors
and glory of His life.

God gave me a new breath. The breath of a new life.
The breath of the Holy Spirit.
Now I am able to breathe again.

The breath has filled my soul with new air.
It allows me now to speak the joy
and abundance of my heart, the glory of God.
From my breath has come the glory
of God's manifestation.

BREATHE AGAIN

My soul was dead to me, but now is alive to Jesus.
The breath has come with God's virtues and gifts.
They are manifested in His glory.
With my breath I moved from the natural
to a place of holiness and righteousness
with the peace of the Lord.

I was given a new breath,
a new life, a new beginning from God.
A new breath for me to breathe again.

PRAYER CHANGES THINGS

Pray daily to the Lord.
Talk with Him and you will understand:
Prayer does change things, but only by His will.
He changes them for you.

Praying daily the prayer of our Father
is pleasing to His ear.
Asking for what is on your heart
is the honesty that He wants to hear.
Speaking to Him in your own words
is coming to know Him.

Know your conversation and you will know God.
Understand that when you pray,
God already knows what you are praying for.
God wants you to ask, to seek, to understand,
so you will know His love.

As you pray, know that God is in control:
in control of your heart, words, and deeds,
in control of your will.
Praying is talking daily to the Father.
He wants you to talk with Him.
He wants you to know Him in your life.
God wants you to invite Him into your life.

PRAYER CHANGES THINGS

Know that you will not always get what you seek.
You will not always get what you see.
You will not always get what you desire.
Only those things that God has willed will you receive.
Only those things,
which God places on your heart to help others know Him,
will He bestow on you.

Pray daily to the Lord.
Talk with Him and you will understand:
Prayer does change things, but only by His will.
He changes them for you.

LIFE STRINGS

The chords are beautiful when harmoniously played
at the right time.
The music is so beautiful to My ear.

Just as the strings of the harp or violin when touched by the hand
that plays, so too do the chords sound melodious tones.
So too does your life and the ways you live, for nothing happens in
your life without the touch of My hand
upon the strings of your heart.

Your life lived day after day is like the sounding strings
of a harp or violin.
I touch the strings of the chord to sound
when you are to listen.
I touch the strings of the chord to sound
when you are to speak.
I touch the strings of the chord to sound
when you are to obey and love others.

The more I play the chords,
the more you learn of Me and My ways,
the more you learn of yourself
and the life of your Lord,
the more you are prepared for things
that come your way and the way of others.

LIFE STRINGS

The strings are touched in place so you may learn and be guided
through your life.
As you hear the notes of your chord,
you will remember all that has been taught to you
through your life.

The strings of your life have been touched
by My hand,
the chords sound beautiful notes.
It is the music of your life.
It is soothing and pleasing to My likeness.
It is the music of a life of Christ,
a life full of learning and love.

Your life strings have been so beautifully touched
by Me, and sound pleasing to My heart.

GIVING MAKES YOU RICHER

Give of yourself to others in need.
Know that you are here for their needs
and also their need of God.
God has given you enough love in your heart
to share with many others.
Do as you are commanded.

Do not hold onto your love
like a thief hoarding treasures.
Give the love that was given to you.
Give all of yourself and your ways to others;
have others in your thoughts first.

A king when pleased
will give away His many treasures.
He will bestow properties, gifts, and jewels
to reward those who have pleased Him.
So too is the Lord, your King,
who has given you many blessings and love.
You have pleased the Lord;
give your gifts to others in need.
When others receive your gifts of love and blessings,
their lives will change forever.
They will be filled with Christ's love,
and they will share it with many others.

GIVING MAKES YOU RICHER

There are those who do not know the love of Christ.
It is you who must make them know.
It is you who must give, so they can share with others.
It is you who has been rewarded and will again
be rewarded for your giving.

Give of your inner self to those in need of His righteousness
and everything will be made pure and clean for you.
Do these things in the name of Jesus Christ,
and the riches of the Lord's kingdom will be given to you.
No thief will be able to touch them.
You will be rich as a king,
but only through your giving can this be done.

For what you give on earth,
the Lord will give back to you in His kingdom.
What you squander,
the Lord will take from you tenfold.

JESUS IS SEARCHING

He moves from door to door, person to person,
place to place.
He is searching and looking inside and out.
He is looking for His character,
looking where His love belongs.
He is looking at your heart, and He is looking for a place
to call home.

He walks among us; He talks to us, He listens
and lives with us.
He is found in the most unusual places and people,
but only those with the heart of Jesus can see
and feel Him.

It is you He is looking for so that He may rest
and you may become the place for His home.

Love of His sharing trickles from His heart.
The walk of His caring is with every footstep He makes.
Touch Him; feel Him; walk with Him.

As you speak and touch others, so will He.
Be not afraid of any you touch or speak with,
for Jesus will protect you.

JESUS IS SEARCHING

He is moving and searching,
always searching for His love in some way or form
through a heart showing His mercy and His love.

He is searching, searching for you.
Let Jesus find you and give you rest.
Become the place for His home.

KNOCK AT THE DOOR

Why do you call Me Lord if you are not doing
what I want you to do?
Why do you call Me Lord if you are not hearing
what I am saying?
Why do you ask for guidance if you will not follow
My commands, which I have given?

Do you know what I have given of My Word,
or do you just hear and not listen?
Do you understand the Spiritual Truth?

Why do you cry out for Me
if you do not listen to what I have to say?
Why do you ask Me to come into your heart,
when you know that I cannot stay in an ungodly place?
One that is filled with hatred and envy of others.
Why do you say My name on your lips and not live
as I have preached?

Ask yourself these questions and answer them
truthfully with the love of God in your reply.
When you call, I will answer and come into your life
only when you speak with a truthful heart,
one filled with the love of Me.
A heart that knows My ways and is willing to follow
in the footsteps of the righteous.

KNOCK AT THE DOOR

When you can truly answer and obey My Word,
then I will come knocking at your door.
I will enter into your house,
the house for My holy body in your life.
There I will rest and remain with you in peace and love
all the days of your life.

HOUSE OF THE LORD

Not made of sticks or stones or mortar,
not a physical structure,
not a place of gold or exquisite furnishings,
just a place for resting with the Lord.

No money can purchase the house.
No carpenter can build it.
No one can give the house to another.
The house must be earned,
earned by the love of a godly hearted person,
earned by a heart pure unto the Lord and others.

The Lord will accept no money, jewels, bargains,
or barter for His house.
The Lord will accept only your unconditional love
as payment for His house.

You can build a house for the Lord only through
your love for Him and others.
The Lord will see a worthy heart.
He will decide if He can rest in your house.

Once you cleanse your heart
and have the Holy Spirit in your soul,
then you can ask the Lord to come into your house.

HOUSE OF THE LORD

Pray to Him and ask,
"Lord, I have built a house for You in my body and soul.
Will you please come in and rest with me?"

He will hear you and come only if He wills it is time.
He will lay down His head with you forever.
He will rest.
It is there He will remain,
in your house that you built for the Lord.

PASTOR

A God-made man of the Word
by My choice.

A man who had not seen,
but now sees.
A man who had not heard,
but is now heard by others.
A man not able to speak to God,
but who now knows the Word of God
and how to speak it to others.

To bring others to the altar of the Lord—that
is your duty.
To bring others to their place in My Kingdom—that
is My calling for you.
To minister to others My Word—that
is My fulfillment.

Carry the message to bring all together
for the glory of your Lord.
Carry the message that God was sent as a gift for all.
Tell of the times of My coming, and
they will understand.
Tell of the times I will be with them,
if they will just obey and believe.
I give you this duty. Perform it well,
and you will see My works at your hands.

PASTOR

Others will know of the truth of your heart
and know that God brought you to this place.
They will know that you only could have come
to where you are now
through Me.

I chose your path some time ago.
You knew it would not be easy.
You knew that was the way I willed for it to be.
The path was chosen, hard and painful,
so others might see My works.
The love of your Lord was always with you
down your crooked path.

You have obeyed and followed.
You will be rewarded always; you already have been,
for your life is full of Me,
and I am in you, always in love.

Lamb of God, minister of Christ,
teacher of the Word, giver of the Life,
Christ's leader for many,
that is you,
always in My heart,
a Pastor.

BRING THEM HOME

Bring My sheep home.
They will be provided to Me upon My coming.
Bring them home with My grace and mercy.

Let them ask for their blessings.
Hear their pleas from their hearts.
You will know I have placed that plea on their hearts
for you to hear.
Speak the words as I give them to you to speak.
Bless all of them in Jesus' name.

Let not their hearts be troubled as you speak for Me.
They will cry for help; My grace and mercy I will bestow
on them through your tongue.
The words they hear will turn their ears and hearts toward Me.

They are waiting to hear a Word.
I speak to some to speak to others; do this for Me.
You have asked for My duty;
serve Me well and bring them home.
They are waiting for Me,
but waiting to hear from Me through you.

Step forward in your faith in Christ.
Step out in your Lord's name.
I want more to come home than to stay out.
Bring them home to their Father.

BRING THEM HOME

Gather them in the love of their Lord.
Speak as I speak to you;
write as I speak to you through the Word.
Let My spiritual tongue be upon you.

So close to home, close to My heart,
bring My sheep back to My fold.
Bring them home.

(Yes, Lord. I will.)

FROM ONE MOTHER TO ANOTHER

Hail Mary, Mother of God,
hear this plea as I pray this prayer to you.
A prayer from a mother's heart.
A prayer that needs no understanding
from another mother.
A prayer for the acknowledgment of God
in her children's lives.

Dear Mary, as I pray to you,
please ask your Son to hear the pleas
from another mother.
Let Him hear and come into my children's lives
to fulfill and guide their ways.
Let them know He is in their lives.
Let Him make known His ways to them,
only in ways they can understand.
Help them in their times of need,
for He knows all their needs.

All are in need of God's love in their lives.
Some of them are in need of guidance.
Some need their ways to be made known to them.
Some need compassion.
Some need to obey His laws.
Some need wisdom and understanding.
Some need inspiration, and others need comfort.

FROM ONE MOTHER TO ANOTHER

They are children of mine,
but they are Your children, Lord.
Show them the way, Lord. Let them know Your love,
the same love You have shown Your mother,
the same love Your mother has shown for You.
The same love this mother has shown Your mother
as I pray for her to hear my pleas.

Please, Mary, Mother of God, hear my plea.
Pray my prayer and let Jesus your Son hear it from you.
Let Him hear me also as I pray, "I ask for these things, pleading from my heart, in Your name, Jesus Christ, amen."

Then, Mother of God, be full of grace, woman,
as you pray with me.
He will know it is a prayer
that comes from the love of a mother's heart.
He will understand,
and He will listen as a child listens
for His mother's voice.
He will know the prayer is a plea,
from one mother to another.

GO LOOKING FOR GOD

Turn me, Lord. Turn me around.
Turn me on the path to go.
Turn me around and out of my troubles.
Turn me from the negatives,
and turn me to trust in You.
Do not let my seed be sown in a negative way.
Let my seed prosper and grow.

(His Response)

Your seed of righteousness is blessed.
I will take the evil and turn it around into good for you.
Look inward to your soul in the unseen world,
with eyes of faith and victory,
and see what good you can see.
Stay filled with hope in My Word.

I am working in your life; look beyond your realm.
Look for the stone, the One who was rejected.
I am the cornerstone of your life.
I am your Mason, the One who cut and molded your fittings for My place.
The One who fit the stone into your life.

GO LOOKING FOR GOD

You are who you are for a reason, My reason.
You are formed by My love to grow into My likeness.
If you listen to the Holy Spirit within you,
you will turn around to Me.
Face not your aggressors, for they are your enemies.
Turn your face to Me.
As the victor, I will keep you safe and protect you.

If you turn toward your Lord,
by My spirit,
you will not have to go looking for God.
You will know that you have already found Me.

THE BRIDEGROOM

I will shed my moonlight on you
like My love shining down upon earth.
The moonlight of My wedding feast
will surround you in My love.
I am the Bridegroom,
and the moon of love is My gift of giving.

The moon is My wedding to earth.
My light shines through the moonlight
unto My people upon the earth.

Be prepared for the feast of My coming.
It will be as a wedding feast
in expectation of the Bridegroom.
Yet those caught up in their own needs
will miss the celebration.
Only those prepared and waiting for My love
will I allow to enter in My wedding celebration,
the celebration of My joining with the people of My love.

The moon is of My making for all to see
the light of Christ always in their lives.
Let My light shine through you,
just as moonlight shines throughout the earth.

THE BRIDEGROOM

"Wait...Wait for Me.
I am your Lord,
your Bridegroom here on earth
and life everlasting."

For I command the light to shine,
to reflect from Me the moon unto you.
I have shown My glory;
I have covered Myself with glory;
I will cover you with glory.
Your glory-filled body
will work toward a precise moment.
It is for that time, not now, that you work and prepare,
which exceeds in the abundance of My glory.

The eye does not physically see the glory of God,
but it is eternal, just as moonlight shines upon you,
seen but not seen,
as an eternal light of Christ,
as the glory of Me,
as the love of your Bridegroom.

THE WAYS OF A BLESSED WOMAN

The ways of a blessed woman are known to God.
The ways are understood and not questioned;
she is guided and not led astray.
These ways are given by God and received by
the blessed woman.

(God Speaking)

Are these your ways?
Are they not the ways I have taught and preached to all?
My ways are given not just to man, but to woman too.
The ways I have shown to you, have you seen and learned?
Can you answer Me?

The blessed woman knows when to show compassion
and care for others.
Knows when to accept others as they are
and not waggle her tongue about them.
Knows how to understand the Word of the Lord
and follow His ways.
Knows how to think of others first before herself.

THE WAYS OF A BLESSED WOMAN

Knows how to speak the Word, follow the Word,
and live her life in the Word made known to her.
Knows how to speak only in the good name of God.
Knows she is not without sin
and will not cast down others; she knows her own faults.
Knows to take the pain of others for her Lord
and carry their burdens to ease their pain.

Are these your ways?
The ways are hard and weary, cumbersome and tiring,
rewarding and uplifting.
The ways are looked upon by My Father,
as blessings given just by Him.

Are these your ways?
"Yes Lord," you answered.

Then you are a blessed woman of Mine.
For you would not answer Me and let your answer
come from your heart if it were not true.

You then understand the ways,
and you will follow them.

Are you a blessed woman?
Yes, you are.

I know the way I want you to live and go through life.
Be faithful to My Word.
I will bestow many blessings on you
as you live the ways of a blessed woman.

INTERTWINED IN THE HEART OF JESUS

Woven together in love,
bonded together by the heart of Christ.
Unto Me you are as one, precious in my giving life.

My heart shows lovingly through the eyes of one.
Cast your gaze upon Me,
know of My love and plans for one.
Know of My spiritual truth.
I have given you three of the One.
You have unity of one through the heart of Jesus.
There is but one flock, and through one Shepherd
you are bonded together in My love.

Intertwined is your life,
connected together in the love of your Lord.
Connected by My plan and My coming into your life.
You are of My spiritual family,
connected by your belief and love of Me.
It is My spiritual family who will last forever.
You are in a spiritual relationship with each other,
and unto Me all will come.

It is of My doing that you were placed in your positions,
and all belong to Me.
Interwoven in one body with My peace on your heart,
you I have called to be one in Me.

I have called each of you together for My coming,
each so precious to Me in My plan,
woven together in place to form the patterns of My life.
Woven together by My hand to share in My pains, sorrows,
woes, joy, hope, peace,
and in love of each other and of Me.

Woven as twine, twisted as a braid—
that is your life in Me.
Threads of understanding, wisdom,
and woe—that is the makeup of your life.
Twine of love, peace, and caring—
that is the makeup of your heart.

Those threads and twine are woven through My heart.
I have woven each of you into My body.
Threads of different colors, when separate,
are just colored threads,
but when woven together, they produce
such a beautiful piece displaying My life.

Each of you is a strand in the making of My plan.
Understand and acknowledge your uniqueness,
your unique strands.
If you are able to do this, you will understand My plan.
You will experience life together and My life,
meant to be shared as one.

Patterns are plentiful,
but this pattern is special in My design,
and you are special to each other.
Each of you is important to the pattern
of the woven cloth of My life.

One strand without the other
cannot complete the pattern of this woven life,
which I have planned for you.
Remember you are woven together in the heart of Christ,
intertwined in My love.

A pattern not seen by all, but seen by My heart.
A pattern not visible to the human eye,
but visible to My eye.
Remain with one another for the making of My plan.
Enjoy the life I have placed before you.
Each of you bonded together in a place and time
in your life for Me.
Preciously placed at the crossroads of your life,
paths meant to be crossed for a reason and purpose,
that is My doing for you.

Each in My heart, woven in love,
hearts bonded together as one in Me…
in Jesus' heart.

GATHERED IN LOVE

All of God's people are given the same blessings.
It is your choice to accept or reject the blessings.
The same rain falls on the tares
as falls on the wheat; both are in need of rain
in order to grow.
Both are gathered at the same time,
the time of God's choosing.

The choices you make let God know which group
He will separate you into, for He knows all.
Will you be in the tares or in the sheaves of wheat?
Only the choices you make in life
will determine God's decision;
it will be determined by your faith.

God will gather the tares and the wheat;
He will separate them into two groups.
The tares will be burned, and the sheaves of wheat
will be gathered close to His heart.

Choose wisely and receive the inheritance
that God has waiting for you.
Your faith will show your choice.
Will you be gathered as tares to be thrown out
or as sheaves of wheat held close to His heart?

Gathered together in the time of His blessings.
Gathered together in His love.
As you remain in God,
you will be as the sheaves of wheat
gathered in God's love close to His heart.

SEED OF LIFE

Your life is a preparation for My journey.
I have instilled My seed in you, the seed of Christ.
You must nourish the seed for it to grow.
You must water the seed and give it food for growth.

The water is My Word;
My ways are its nourishment.
The growth is your life living as Me.
You in Me and Me in you,
that is the seed of life.

I have given you conditions for your life.
I have given you My seed.
I have ordered conditions with you
so that My seed might grow.
I have bestowed on you My giving.
Take, and do what must be done.
Know what I want you to do.

The seed will not wither, but grow in the spiritual light.
The north and south winds will test the seed.
Only with the Holy Spirit will the seed stand the test and
stay strong and grow.
Only in times of the strong cold winds
will the spiritual growth go forward.
Only in your times of trouble will the seed grow stronger.

Do not let the winds wear down My seed.
It will sprout forth a life of Christ,
One of character and conduct like Mine
so that I will always see you in My heart.

SEED OF LIFE

If you follow the way the seed is to grow,
if you obey, the seed will blossom with My passion.
Feel the passion of My love.
Let My nourishment take hold of you.
Feel the beauty of My earth.

Think not of yourself;
give up your childish ways of thinking.
Think of others first and grow with My seed in you
as a soldier of Mine.
I want you as part of My army,
My army of love and protection against all evil.

I have given My seed.
Will you take and bury the seed and not let it grow,
or will you nourish, water, and protect it
so My spirit may grow in you?
Will you hoard the seed like servants hoarding talents?
Some bury them, others invest them for growth;
which will you do?

I will judge and see.
Do not disappoint Me when I come asking
what you have done with the seed.
I gave My seed for a reason and purpose, My purpose.
Take My seed and grow.
Let My seed take root and grow in you.
Make it pleasing to My heart, My eyes,
your soul, and Me.

WISDOM CAN WAIT

Do not let your flesh command you.
Do not let it rule your life.
You are not to live by emotions alone.
You are to live by your wisdom and understanding.
Do not let your emotions come between you
and My wisdom.

Do not give into your flesh.
Your flesh is of a human form.
The spirit of Me is of your soul and lasting life.
The life of the flesh is death,
but not as you know of it in its human form.

Do not let the weakness of your flesh blind your mind.
Let your mind be a spiritual one of reasoning and understanding.
If it is not,
then wisdom can wait on your mind to develop,
but only when two conditions exist:
reasoning and understanding.
It is then that wisdom will join to form a spiritual mind,
a mind ruled by the Spirit and not emotions,
a mind pleasing to Me.

Obey not fleshly commands,
but spiritual commands.
No flesh shall be glorified in My presence.
Only one who lives through the Spirit
will be glorified in My eyes.

WISDOM CAN WAIT

Seek the wine of wisdom
and taste of the eternal kingdom.
Wisdom can wait until you are ready
in your spiritual form.

Do not let your human weakness keep My wisdom from you.
Wisdom is the path and the way to Me.
Wisdom can wait,
but do you want to keep it waiting?
Reasoning, understanding, and wisdom together joined,
all are as one in My feast.

Your flesh is but transparent.
It is your heart that will command your spirit.
Your wisdom will know the difference.
Your wisdom will know that I will not lead you
against My commands.
I will not lead you to sin; one with wisdom
will know the difference.

Lead with your heart and wisdom will follow.
Wisdom will wait for you.
Find your way.

THE SEASONS

To every time there is a season
A time in your life for God's purpose.
A time for God to change your low to high
for His coming.
A change in the way you see God.
A time God sees that your life must change
in order to receive Him.
A change of the seasons.

A time for you to see that your season is of this earth.
The changing of your season is your realization
that you are not of this earth, but of His kingdom.
It is the time to change the seasons in your life.
A time to know God is here,
but waiting in His kingdom for your coming home.

Only by changing your season can you come home to the Lord.
Your season is low and you must make it high.
Bring it high by overcoming pride and serving
as a humble spiritual servant to the Lord.
Your low valley will become as a mountain,
a high place on which to serve God.
Humble yourself and serve.

THE SEASONS

It is the season to change things in your life.
It is the time for a change.
A time for God to come on to your mountain.
He will see the humbleness of your soul.
He will see the change in your seasons,
and that change will endure forever.

Now is the time, the time in your seasons,
your time to change for the Lord.

WEATHER THE STORM

Lay down your life for Me—not your human form,
but your spiritual form.
Let your spiritual form take on more duties for Me.
Learn to be one of My servants, not servant to Me,
but for Me.

Take My life on and accept the changes that will come.
Take up My shelter and anchor close to
My people around you.

The storm will come and weather hard;
the winds and rain will blow.
Only with the anchor of My people
will you weather the storm.
My people are your base and strength.
As you weather the storm, you will grow stronger
with the strength of your Lord.
You will gain My people's strength
and lay heavy the foundation of your Lord.

Your true friends, those of your Lord,
will strengthen your soul and foundation.
Help others find the pathway to the joy in their souls.

WEATHER THE STORM

The rain will come, and the clouds will blacken;
it will grow darker before the light.
Rely on the support of your foundation;
it will help you weather the storm.
Lay your spiritual foundation
upon the One I have given you.
Build upon it, and it will lead you and My people
to the light that awaits after the storm.

Know your base and foundation.
Lay your spiritual life upon it.
Lay your life upon My spiritual foundation.
Build upon it for others to see,
and they will be able to weather their storms.

STAND FIRM

Stand firm in the strength of the Lord.
You are a child of God standing on the ground
where He has placed you.
The gates of evil cannot overcome you if you stand firm
in the love of the Lord.

Some things will look good and not be good.
Some things will look evil and not be evil.
Do not be blinded by the source.
You will see and know of all things
whether good or evil
with the faith and strength of the Lord.
Do not become confused.
Know your source of power, that which is given to you
from the love of the Lord.

Walk and talk in the spirit.
Pray and obey the Lord, and your feet will be planted
firm in faith.
You are already a child of God,
which gives you the strength of the Lord.
The strength has been infused into you.
Know of it and become self-sufficient in the Lord.

Stand firm, stand firm, stand firm,
resist and stand firm.

STAND FIRM

Trust the Lord, surrender your soul;
you will be able to stand up against all evil.
You will know you have the ability already
to withhold all evil.
This power has already been given to you from the cross.

Pray for your strength and that of others
so they will not be led astray.
Pray that they will know of their strength
if they just trust in the Lord.

The love of the Lord will prevail.
Do not give up; do not falter or fall.
You cannot, knowing you have the trust of the Lord
with you.

Give all of yourself and worship with your heart.
Your prayers will release the power of God to stand with you against
the forces of evil.

Stand firm, stand firm, stand firm,
resist and stand firm.

You will know the strength of the Lord is with you.

CHOOSE WISELY

The choices you make reflect upon your life.
Is it a life that you want to display to Christ?
Is it a life you wear upon your heart?
Is it one you want Christ to be pleased with and proud of?

The choice is yours.
Your free will was given by God's choosing,
a choice He chose so wisely for you.
Will your choice be as wise,
or will it be as the snare of the fowler?

Your choice will give you the inheritance you desire.
Will your inheritance be the kingdom of God,
or will it be like one of a lost sheep,
always looking for the shepherd's way home?
The life of Christ is not easily followed,
but it is one with many rewards.

The choice you make will be made by your heart,
not by your thinking.
The Lord will decide the inheritance for you.
Only by His doing are all things possible and believable.
Only by His doing will He decide the weight
of your inheritance.

You were invited into this life to live for the inheritance.
Live it and choose wisely.
Receive the abundance He has waiting for you.
Only according to your life choices
will God make His decision.

Confirm your choices through your heart,
not by mental conception.
You are an heir of God through Christ;
live for your inheritance.
The choice of your inheritance is yours;
choose wisely.

THE FILES

They are as clear as black and white;
there is no gray in between.
They are the files of good and evil;
there is no in between.

You must choose the files in your life.
You must make the choice between good and evil,
for your choices are recorded on tablets
and kept in files in the Lord's house.

On the day of judgment God will pull your tablets
and look upon your files.
What will they contain?
Will your files be filled with shame, ways of the flesh,
and earthly things?
Or will your files contain deeds of goodness,
love of others, and ways of serving
Him and His people?

Every step, thought, word you speak,
and action you take in your life is recorded
on the tablets in your files.
If you have the heart of Christ in you,
your file will contain more good than evil.
If you have a contrite heart,
your tablets will be blackened with the stains
of evil thoughts and acts.

THE FILES

What do you want the Lord to see?
When He is beside you looking at your files,
what do you want to feel?
Shame or happiness, guilt or peace?

The files are filled by you;
your life places markings on your tablets.
Every day you write upon the tablets; unknown to you,
the recordings are being made.
The recordings began even before your birth.
The files of your life were prepared by the Lord;
He named your files.
He already knows what is on the tablets.
He knows what marks you will make.
He knows all. He is God.
He has already chosen whose tablets He will cover
with His name, the name of Jesus.

Jesus will judge your tablets and cover your files with His blood,
writing His name across them.
This will only be done if He chooses to find them worthy of
His covering.

Where? Where are your files?
Are they ready for the Lord's review?
Are you ready for the Lord to look upon you?
Good or evil, God believer or non-believer,
what choices have you made?
What markings are you recording?
Where are you in your life with God in your files?

Rethink what God has given you.
The day you stand in the house of the Lord
with your files is coming.
Your tablets you cannot hide,
for He knows all things.
Please the Lord with your files.
Do not worry about the evil stains on them;
He knows those stains are there.
He knows all will have some evil stains
throughout their lives,
but let the good marks outnumber the evil stains,
and He will cover your files with His name.

Where will you be on that judgment day with the Lord?
Will you be standing before Him
or trying to hide from Him because of your shame?

The files are yours to make.
Stand before the Lord with your life files
in His name.

WASH ME, LORD

Wash away the guilt of my sins.
Cleanse my soul for You.
Take my offenses from me, Lord.
Clean my heart of hardness.
For I know only a clean heart can accept You
and Your Spirit.
Cleanse my soul for Your Spirit to enter.
Cleanse my heart and wash away my transgressions.

(His Response)

Call upon Me, and your soul will be clean.
I will wash your guilt away,
because you have asked it to be done.
I will cleanse your body of your iniquities.
You are pure and will be able to enter My kingdom.
My cleansing will not put out the fire in your heart.
The flame will remain burning for My love,
an eternal flame yearning for My Holy Spirit.

My washing will renew and refresh your soul.
You will feel the warmth of My love in your life.
You will be a flame-bearing minister.
The flame will remain kindled in your heart;
there too I will remain with you,
always as the flame of My Spirit.

MESSENGERS OF GOD

We are as stars in the night that God has flung into the sky.
We are the light of Christ to lead others home to Him.
When things appear dark, it is the stars of the night that will shine brightest in these times.

We are Christ-believers, Christ-servants,
Christ-bearers, Christ-givers; we are His children.

We have a duty to provide light to those in darkness,
to those in their own distress, to those in need of God.
We must shine the path for them to walk
into the eternal light, to bring them closer to God's home.

When it appears to grow dark then grossly darker,
it is then we perform our duty.
It is then we shine brighter than ever,
just like the morning star.
We bring the message of Christ to those in the dark,
to those who have forgotten Him, to those in despair.

We are messengers of the Light, the Light of Christ.
We are prophets of a future kingdom
not seen or understood by all.
Our duty will never be complete, our tasks will never end.
Just as the stars always shine light,
we too will shine God's light on His people.
We are God's warriors to protect those in need.

MESSENGERS OF GOD

"Make us strong, Lord;
please make us strong to carry your message."

Through the night the stars shine light,
and we will be as God's stars on earth.
Messengers of His love and Word,
guardians of the gate,
keepers of His house,
always waiting for Him to call on us to deliver a message
to someone needing His love.

We are messengers,
messengers through the night,
waiting to shine His light on the path home,
delivering His love and His light.

THY FOOTSTEPS HAVE BEEN ORDERED

Know thy footsteps;
the steps of the righteous are ordered.
See the pathway I have placed before you;
know your heart, your true heart.

Are your footsteps ordered?
What pathway have you chosen?
Is it different from the one that I have chosen for you?
Do you know the way—My way?
You said you know your way and will follow My voice.
Is that a man speaking after his own heart or Mine?
Do you speak from your mind and not your heart?
Do you speak with a false tongue
and talk as a false prophet?
Do you speak with a split tongue?
Speak with one tongue,
and speak the truth to your Lord.

Know your way is My way and follow My voice.
You cannot go wrong.
I have ordered your footsteps.
I have called you to step forward.
Take your step in Me and question Me not.
If you do not come when I call, you have not obeyed.

THY FOOTSTEPS HAVE BEEN ORDERED

Do you know how to listen for My voice,
know of My Word, feel and feed of it?
If you do, you will hear My voice calling you.
If you do not hear My voice,
then you are not ready to walk forward in My Word.

Will you ever be ready?
Or will you stay in the comfort of your place?
Not My place, but the one you chose with your mind.
I will stand with the righteous.
I will walk with the righteous every step
of their way.
I have called and ordered.

Will you walk with Me?
Your footsteps will be taken with Me;
you cannot fall; I will not let you.
Step forward in My Word.
I have left the formation of My Father's footsteps
for you to follow.
Come forward; you will know the way.
Though you can only see one set
of footsteps,
there will always be two: yours and Mine.

Walk forward in My calling.
Do not fear, for I am with you.
Come and step forward with Me.

NEW WINE

Shed your old wineskin when Jesus comes.
You will not be able to hold the Holy Spirit in your old wineskin,
your old life, when you accept the Lord.

Take on your new wine, the Holy Spirit,
in a new wineskin.
Burst forth with the Spirit of the Lord
and pour it on His people.
Burst from your old wineskin to a new life in Christ.

When you take on the Holy Spirit,
you will become as new wine.
Just as the water was changed into new wine,
so too will you be changed.

Be as new wine, a new life, a new beginning.
New wine of the Holy Spirit must have new wineskins.
New wine poured into old wineskins will burst.
The wine will spill and the skins will tear.
So too will your life
if you do not change your wineskin.

Become dead to the old and take on the new way of life,
the life of Christ, the life of the Holy Spirit.

NEW WINE

New wine is fresh, pure in taste, and sweet smelling.
It bursts forth in a new, rich flavor.
Your life will be as a new wine
when you accept the Lord Jesus in your life.
God's glory and grace-giving gifts will grow in you.
Let others taste of your new wine and want to thirst for more
from the Winemaker.
Let them thirst for new wine to fill their wineskins.

Pray,
"Lord, let the new wine fill my new wineskin.
Let it fill and stretch my skin, preserving the wine so others
may taste the Word of You. Holy Spirit, come fill my life,
fill my new wineskin. Let others taste of the Word and
know the sweetness and the glory of You. Let the wine make
them happy with the joy of You. Let me be as a new vessel
for the Lord's use—a new vessel to hold new wine, the
new life I have received from You. Let nothing satisfy this
filling of my wineskin except the gift of Your Holy Spirit."

Nothing will satisfy you except the taste of Jesus,
the taste of the Holy Spirit, the taste of His new life,
the taste of a new wine.

THE MIRROR

Afraid to look, afraid of what you will see?
Afraid of your future,
because you can't let go of your past?
That is you, a scared, innocent child of Mine.

Your life has been one filled with many disappointments,
but I have filled it with many joys also.
You have held onto the troubling times and
do not know how to let go to the joyous times.
They have all been given by Me to you,
all in your growing to reach Me,
all in your coming to the way of your Lord.

You think if you let go you will be lost,
but a shepherd does not leave even one sheep alone.
You think I have not heard you,
but it is you who have not heard Me.

You know I am there, but you keep turning away.
Sooner than you think you will turn to your Lord.
Sooner than you think
you will have to look at the person in the mirror,
and when you do, you will see Me
standing right beside you.

THE MIRROR

Suffer no more; look in the mirror;
see who is looking back at you.
You will see the life you have longed for,
but thought you never could have.
You will see your Savior.
Just trust in Me and look in the mirror.

Painful at first, lonely will you feel,
but call My name, Jesus, and see Me in the mirror,
the mirror of your life.
It is My life also, for if you look you will see Me in you,
but first you must look.

Walk in My life, give of yourself to Me
as you have given of yourself to others on earth.
I am now waiting for your time,
and you will experience all My joys,
which I have to give you.

Look in the mirror; look there for Me
and let go of your old life.
You are called, and you are a child of Mine.

When you look in the mirror,
you will be looking not at you,
but you will finally be seeing Me.

OINTMENT OF THE LORD

Our souls are chafed from the stains of our sins.
The rubbings of guilt and evil are as sores upon us.
There is only one healing for that ailment.
It is the ointment of the Lord.

Let your ointment pour over us, Lord; give us relief.
The ointment of the Lord will be abundant, soothing, healing,
but gentle to the touch of our souls.

The Lord is the ointment;
His name alone is an ointment poured forth.
Just as a good measure, pressed down, shaken together,
and poured forth,
so is the name of the Lord.

As you go forward with your ointment,
it will continue to soothe your chafed soul.
Do not let the piercing of evil sore your soul.
Use the ointment of the Lord.
It will soothe your pain.

The fragrance of the ointment
is overwhelming to the soul.
The smell of the ointment is sweet and drawing,
an aroma that fills the air and soothes the soul.
Breathe of the scent; let it fill your soul
and heal the scars.

OINTMENT OF THE LORD

It is breathtaking; it is the ointment of the Lord,
calming and healing in His giving.

Heal our souls, Lord, measure and pour down upon us
Your ointment of love.
Heal our chafed souls, for we are tired of Satan tempting us
with evil and earthly ways.
Soak our souls with your ointment, Lord;
saturate us with your Spirit.

Heal us with Your ointment, Lord;
then anoint us with Your love.
Anoint us with Your blessing to be one with You.
Let us feel soothed in the love of Your name.

JOURNEY TO THE LORD

It can be long or short.
It can be one that started years ago
or one that started yesterday.
It is one filled with despair, joy, confusion,
love, and peace in the Lord.
It can be wandering and winding
through the lives of people,
a journey that we walk to the Lord.

You may feel that God has been there with you
all along your way, or you may feel
that you never knew Him.
You have been searching and seeking
all along the way of the journey.
There are times when you felt so alone
that you did not feel His presence in your life.

The road at times has been lonely and dark,
difficult to walk.
It has not been easy to follow the footsteps
of the Lord, but it has been rewarding.
A journey filled with laughter and pain,
but one that you never regret you have come through,
when you find your place in the Lord.

JOURNEY TO THE LORD

There is so much love along the way.
Look back over your shoulder and see
the path you have walked.
You are a follower of Christ.
Take hold of the Lord's hand.
He will guide you on His journey.
When you walk with the Lord, you will see
the wonders of His way.
Visions and glory will lie at your feet;
they will be given to you along the journey.

At the end of the journey,
you will be at the door of His kingdom.
You will enter only with your spirit and soul.
Walk in His garden; feel His beauty and love,
know of His heart.

Yes, the journey to the Lord is long, hard, painful,
not easy, but ever so joyfully rewarding.

Touch the people He wants you to touch.
Speak to the people He wants you to speak with;
speak His Word.
Love the people He wants you to love.
Listen not to others as they speak harshly against you;
let not their words turn your ear.
Listen only to the heart of the Lord;
it will guide you on your rewarding journey.
His heart will light the way.

Enter into His kingdom from your journey,
and you will hear your Father say,
"Welcome home."

THE INWARD VOICE

Speak to me Lord; let me hear Your voice upon my heart.
I long to hear the voice I have grown so accustomed to.
The voice that sounds like no other, so soft in tone and gentle
in speaking; the voice is Yours, Lord.

I heard the inward voice in me
only when I turned my life over to the Lord.
I confessed, repented, and gave into Your will,
and an inward voice began to speak to me.

It is a voice as no other. Once you hear it,
you will want to hear it more.
You will want the Lord to speak to you always.
You await the voice, and you want to please and serve
and do whatever the voice has you do.

A sound like no other sound on earth is the voice of the Lord.
Much understanding and love come with that voice.
Once the voice speaks to you, all the wisdom, knowledge, peace,
and love that He wants you to have is given to you.

Give yourself to the Lord.
Listen for His voice to speak to you.
You will be filled with the Holy Spirit
once the voice falls on your ears and heart.
The voice is heard with the heart, not the head.

THE INWARD VOICE

Do not be mistaken about what you hear.
Do not confuse the voice of the world
with the inward voice.
The voice of the Lord is the inward voice.
The voice of the Lord is anointed and audible
only to your heart.

Hear it; feel it; live it.
Let His love fill your heart as He speaks to you.
Let your heart accept the voice
and do whatever He commands.
The inward voice will come to all,
but not all will come to it.
The inward voice speaks,
but not all hear and not all listen.

Repent, confess, and give in to the Word of God.
Let your will become His will and then listen as He speaks
to you from the inward voice.

THE PAINTBRUSH OF THE LORD

A branch taken from His tree of life, His vine,
and used for many purposes.

The Lord has chosen one of His branches from His tree.
He uses the branch to touch others.
The branch speaks to others in need of Him.

The branch tells of His life and of belonging to His tree.
The story of being a twig:
growing throughout life to become a branch of beauty,
but only with the nourishment and feeding of the vine.

It is a branch dipped in the wine of His blood
and used as a paintbrush in the lives of people He wants
to touch.

The colors are beautiful
as they flow on the canvas of life.
The faces and lives of people change with the paintings from the
dipping of the wine…
like being covered with His blood.

THE PAINTBRUSH OF THE LORD

The colors are yellow, red, white, and hues
of many nations, many people, but all faces of Christ.
All colors bridge the gap with God's paintbrush,
for as it is in heaven, that is the way it will be on earth.
Beautiful colors of many faces
created only by the vine.
For the branch of His vine, He dips into His wine
and shares the color for all to see His love.

As you partake in God's wine and walk in His life,
you paint a picture as you go.
Your branch has touched the Lord's paint,
His blood rich in color.

Let your life play out as a paintbrush in His painting.
Brush out to those in need of Him
and touch those who need His color.
Complete His portrait of life,
as the paintbrush of His vine of many colors.

GIVE ME THE DRINK, LORD

My soul is thirsting for Your love,
thirsting for Your Word,
thirsting to be near to You, My Lord.

Quench my thirst with Your spirit, Lord.
Let Your spirit touch me, and let my parched soul
be filled with the water of the Holy Spirit.

Let the water flow from me as a river to others,
Your Word of Christ.
Let the water flow so others may know of You.

Give me the drink, Lord. Give me Your spirit.
Let me feel the satisfaction of the drink,
as cool water flowing on a hot day.
Let the Word come upon me and refresh my need
of You, Christ.

Let me give of Your drink, Lord.
Let me pass it on to others.
Let me give your Word, Lord, so their thirst may
be quenched as You have quenched mine.

Dear Lord, give me the water—water of Your Word.
Let me have more and more until it runs over me,
through me, and from me.

GIVE ME THE DRINK, LORD

Give me the drink, Lord.
Soothe my dry bones and revive them for You.
Let them be as new.

Let the water flow from my mouth and tell
the glories of You, and all will know You are the Lord,
the Giver of the drink.

Let others know You are the One holding the cup
as they drink of Your water.
Quench our soul, Lord; then quench some more.
Let us drink only when You, our Father, gives,
knowing the amounts we need to swallow
to be near to You and to soothe our soul.

Give me the drink, Lord.
Quench my parched and chafed soul.
Fill my thirst; fill me with Your spirit.
Fill me with the drink of Your love.

WATER OF THE WORD

The Word of God flows like water among the rocks.
Just as water flows from one rock to another,
so too may My Word flow among you and all people.

My Word will flow like water as at the wedding feast
for all to see Me in it.

My Word will trickle out to the lonely and the destitute,
so they too may know My love.

My Word will roar like the water in the ocean,
as I cast down shadows on all sinners
who will not repent and be saved.

My Word will flow as water in a pond on a spring day,
brightening the souls of those waiting for the Lord God,
for theirs is a place in heaven.

Just as the flowing water calms,
so too may My Word quiet the hearts
of the weary souls.

My Word will flow like a stream into a body of water.
That body of water will be My blood and body,
waiting for all to partake of it and become one in Me.

WATER OF THE WORD

I give the water, water of the Word.
Drink of it and be saved.
I give the Word; take of it and know the way.
I give to all the water of the Word;
many will not be able to drink,
but those who do drink will thirst no more
and will know Me in them forever.

WHIRLWIND

As a man comes and goes,
so too does his life as he walks and changes.

Just as a whirlwind,
the man who passes through the wind of the earth
and My ways will not be the same man who entered
into the wind.
The man will come out of the wind a changed man of Mine
as he walks with the light of his Lord.

Swaying in the breeze will his life be,
as he draws near to Me.
As caught by the wind and tossed to and fro, so too are
his thoughts and life as he is led by My Spirit.

Circling, circling,
round and round,
man not knowing to look up or down.
Circling, circling, to and fro,
always around and down it goes.
Deep into your heart and out to man,
it is the love of Your Lord
and the wind of the land.

WHIRLWIND

Changed is the person I meant to change.
Never the same as you were born,
but scattered in love, in My love wind torn.
My love that I once bore just for you,
but now to beseech you back to Me.

The love of My heart in My wind I did scatter
to capture your heart
in the wind of your life and time.

Enter into My whirlwind,
up and down, to and fro.
Scatter My love as far as
you can make it go.

Go in one way, come out anew
but only with My help and love for you.
Holy Spirit, blow your wind into their lives,
set them apart from their previous lives.

Angel of mercy, do not let go.
For I am the One who tossed them to and fro,
to and fro, up and down.
My love is a whirlwind unmistakably known,
twisting and turning, soft and firm to the touch,
never forgetting My love as such.

Enter as one man, but come out another.
Let My wind take your breath away and out of you,
but breathe of My spirit, breathe in the new.

Let My Word take care of you, and let go to the wind
to land where you may, but only with My hand
to lay you gently down on earth,
landing with a new birthing girth.
Girth of the Lord, hold on firm to make you steady
in the whirlwind of love, but only if you are ready.

Hold steadfast and true
in the whirlwind spun just for you.
Hold onto your Lord; stay close to the wind's spirit.
Surround yourself with the love of My spirit.

Do not get caught in the tempest or the storm;
Instead, feel My love in the whirlwind of warm,
everlasting love to be reborn.

PEACEMAKERS

We are God's peacemakers here on earth,
trying to provide a calm, serene, harmonious atmosphere.
We are here to provide His peace to those in need.
Our duty is to give to others the peace He has given to all,
but they have forgotten it is there for their asking.

The peace the Lord gives is not of this world, but His.
His peace is a calming for the soul.
We are servants waiting to please Him and give His peace
and love to others.
We can only talk with others, telling them how to ask Him
for His peace,
for they need guidance for their request.

We are waiting, Lord,
always waiting for Your command to go forward
to the souls needing your peace.
We are your friends, waiting to hear Your command,
waiting to share Your peace with others,
Your peace that you gave to us.

Lord, give us Your pure wisdom from above.
Let us carry that fruit of the seed to others.
Let them know Your peace-loving ways.
Let them yield to Your will, Lord, Your peaceful, gentle touch.
We are waiting, Lord, waiting for Your command
to take Your peace forward.

We will deliver Your Word to others,
so they too will know that You are God.
We will work for Your peace and work to make peace in others.
We will not let them go, Lord.
We will let them know how easy it is for them to have Your
peace if they will just ask You, Lord, from their hearts;
Hearts that must be pure and clean in Christ
just as the wisdom You sent from above.
Peace so easy for their taking and asking,
for You made it so, Lord.

Humble friends are we of Yours, O Lord.
Humble in our asking for You to let us share
Your peace with others.
We will make Your peace in us known to others.

We are Your peace servants, Lord,
but You call us friends.
Let us then carry out Your commands
to give and share peace with others.
Lord, give us Your true Spirit with Your wisdom
to carry out Your commands for You.

Lord, let others know of Your straightforwardness,
Your compassion, and gentle touch
which give them peace in their lives.
Let them feed upon the fruit that provides peace to all.
Lord, let Your harvest be full in prosperity.
Let You, Lord, reap what we have sown for You, for we are Your
friends, Your peacemakers, wanting to do
Your will and please You always.

PEACEMAKERS

Lord, we will only sow what You gave us for our taking,
Your peace and love.
Lord, you gave us Your peace, and we are accepting it,
we are accepting our duty.
We want to share it with others,
so they too will be at harmony and peace in their lives.
Let them know the love of the Lord.
Let us, Lord, fulfill our duty as Your peacemakers,
so others will know how to be one of us for You.

We are God's peacemakers,
following His will of peace,
sharing in His wisdom and His love,
carrying out the commands He has given us.

PERSONAL REFLECTION - INSPIRATION

❖ How has God inspired you?

❖ Now that God's inspiration has touched you, what do you plan to do with this gift?

- ❖ What is the most inspirational thing you have done for someone which included using the Word of God?

____

____

____

____

____

- ❖ How do you plan to use God's inspiration in His plan for you?

____

____

____

____

____

- ❖ What is your plan to inspire others to grow closer to God on a daily, weekly or monthly basis?

____

____

____

____

____

PRAISE

My mouth is filled with Your praise
and with Your glory all day long.

—Psalm 71:8 (NASB)

OH...UPLIFTED IS MY SOUL

How can I not rejoice in the songs of the Lord?
How can I not sing out God's praise?
Listen to the words as they are told from above;
listen to the stories they say.

How can I not be glad and uplifted?
How can I not rejoice?
How can I not sing out to the world,
singing in harmonious voice?

Sing out to the world to bring joy;
Sing out to lift up God's spirit;
Sing out, for the glory of God is around you;
Sing out songs of love for all.

Oh...how glorious are praises to the Lord!
The praises are so glorious
that they make you want to sing inside your soul.
The praises are so glorious
that they make you want to run, not hide.

The praises are so mighty
that you will want to see God.
The praises sing out to God,
asking for His unfathomable love,
His love that He showered from above
so all may love one another as you sing,

Oh...how glorious are the praises to the King!
So glorious that they uplift our souls,
so glorious that they tell of stories told,
of the days when He walked the earth
and showed man the way to go,
of the time the Lord came not to scold,
but to love all for their faults and let them know.
Love one another and sing out and behold.

Oh...uplifted is my soul,
so uplifted that only God can truly know.

TO THINE OWN GLORY BE TRUE

Know yourself, the truth about you.
Give praise and honor to My name;
glorify Me in every way.

Release the life I have given you here on earth
and glorify Me.
Hold on, not to this life, but to the life I
have promised you.
Glorify and praise Me all the days.
Say praises and glory unto My name
and please Me.

Worship Me.
Hold unto Me all that you can give of this life.
Offer thanksgivings to Me and abide in My Word.
If you abide in My Word you will have abundance
of glory and praises from Your Lord.
I have abundance to give you.

Glorify your Lord and say My Holy Name.
Receive My Word.
Many favors will I bestow on you,
favors waiting to be given.
Be truthful to your heart, and you will be truthful
to your Lord.

To My glory give praises and thanksgiving,
and I will give back to you.
Give glory and praises to Me, your Lord, Jesus the Christ.

MINISTER TO CHRIST

He is waiting, waiting for you to ask.
Waiting to hear His name from you,
waiting for you to come to Him.

Minister to Christ first.
Call upon His holy name—Jesus.
Give Him praise and worship.
Give Him glory.
Sing out His name unto Him.
Your first ministry is to minister to your Maker,
then He will minister to you, through you, to others.

Do not perform works of the Lord
before you perform your duties to Him.
Minister to Him in spirit and truth.
His spirit and truth is the Holy Spirit.
By the Holy Spirit can you come to God
and minister to the Lord.

Speak with the tongue of the spirit.
As you pray with the spirit you pray with God.
You cannot come to God without the spirit;
unless He commands.
Seek Him in your heart. He will know your truth;
speak only with the spirit and truth.

MINISTER TO CHRIST

First every morning say,
"Lord, I have come to minister to You first.
I put You first before all others.
Commune with me, Lord, before this day."

He will hear and be pleased.
He will be with you and love you.
You will do your duty unto the Lord.
It will be pleasing to His heart to know that you
have placed Him first;
first in your heart, in your life, in your day and thoughts,
first on your mind, the name of Jesus.

Thank you, Lord, for this day.
This day you gave us to minister first to You.
We will rejoice and be glad in it.

A TEARDROP FROM GOD'S EYE

Do you know how precious God's love is for you?
So near to His heart is a place just for you.
Your love is wrapped around God's heart so tight,
love that He wove into a tapestry of your life.

A tapestry that is more brilliant than the sun
and more precious than gold.
A tapestry that knows sorrow, worry, and woe.
A tapestry that knows peace, happiness, and love.
A cloth so precious that tears fell from above.
God's tears dropped to earth from the heavenly skies;
those teardrops are your life in disguise.

(God Speaking)

Do you know how precious you are to Me?
More precious than birds that sing in the spring.
More precious than dew drops from heaven above.
So precious to Me that My heart strings have tugged.

I say to you, "Will you follow Me?"
You answer, "Yes, Lord," most reverently.
Stay with Me, child, for God knows your fears.
Call on Me always, for I'm always near:
near to provide comfort, to consult and control,
near to give guidance with wisdom for your woes.

Pray for My courage through tough times ahead.
Pray for My guidance down the path you must tread.
Pray to My Father; He will listen to you.
Pray for right choices that you must now choose.

So listen, follow, speak, and sing
the praises of My Father, the King of Kings.
Speak the Word to all who will listen and believe.
Tell of your tapestry so others may see
how precious God's love is for them and thee.

Do you know how precious you are to Me?
More precious than burnished gold and myrrh,
a precious teardrop from God's eye here on earth.

Do you know how precious you are to Me?
"Yes, Lord," you answered most reverently.

JESUS, MY FRIEND

He is everywhere, and He is everything.
He is my Lord and Savior,
my Redeemer and my Maker.
He is my Friend, Jesus.

Talk with Jesus, and He will talk with you.
Talk to Him about His Word, and He will tell you all
He wants you to know.
He will share His life stories and passages with you.

How do you become a friend of Jesus?
You share your feelings with Him.
You talk with Him and trust Him.
You listen to what He has to say and take His Word
into your heart.
You are His friend if you keep His commands.
Your friendship with Jesus will last forever.

He is a good friend, and good friends last forever.
Good friends tell others about their friends.
Friends of Jesus tell their friends about Jesus.
His Word is told and goes forth in a flurry
among good friends.

JESUS, MY FRIEND

Be honest with yourself and you will be honest
with Jesus.
Jesus will be your intimate conversation with the Lord.
He is there listening to all your troubles, taunts,
and tribulations.
As you talk with your friend, Jesus, you talk with God.
Share all your thoughts and secrets with the Lord.
Know your heart is filled with love in the sharing
of His secrets with other true friends.

Jesus, your friend, wants you to come to Him,
to be closer in the friendship.
Even in times of distance, He is with you.
Jesus is always around and will never leave you.

Put your trust and friendship in Jesus,
and it will come back to you.
You will hear His voice and feel His presence.

A friend, walking right beside you,
a friend walking with you,
your friend, Jesus.

CURSE UPON THE CROSS

Jesus was the redeemer of our curse that
we placed upon the cross.
It was by our mouths that He was crucified,
to endure the pain for what we spoke.
It was through our actions and deeds, our forgetting others,
our placing our needs first,
that the curse was born.

The curse, spoken first by man long ago,
is still spoken of today by many unfamiliar
to God and His love.
The curse was made known by man's word of mouth;
the same words that came from our tongue
and placed our Savior on the cross.
By our tongue He did hang;
out of the abundance of the heart our mouth spoke,
and it spoke a curse that Jesus endured for us.

Christ redeemed us from the curse
by being our Redeemer on the cross.
By our own words, we released the ability of the enemy
upon Christ and us.
Christ became our curse to overcome all evil.
It is by His stripes we are saved.

The Word of God in His Spirit controls our tongue
and stops us from casting our shadows among people.
Jesus is the living Word of God
who took our curse upon the cross.

CURSE UPON THE CROSS

(God Speaking)

Speak from your heart with My spirit.
Do not let the words of your mouth snare you.
Do not let your tongue keep you in bondage.
Free yourself with words of praise and worship for Me.

A wholesome tongue is a tongue of life.
Have you a tongue of life?
Your tongue once put Me on the cross for you.
Curse Me not from your tongue,
but praise Me with many worshipping words.
Do not let your tongue bring a curse upon you.
Let your tongue be as the Spirit of My life and your soul.

The heart of the wise teaches his tongue and mouth,
and the lips learn from it.
Blessings and curses should not come out of the same mouth.

If your heart has an abundance of evil,
then curses will flow from your lips.
If your heart has an abundance of good,
then many blessings will flow.

Let My blood cover you and prevent you
from casting curses with your lips.
Your tongue was placed in you for calling
out praises and worship unto Me.
Let your tongue call My name—Jesus.
I redeemed the curse for you;
now become God's child for Me.

RENDER UNTO GOD

Our faith and belief in Christ
are not coins
that we pay for benefits from God.
God purchased our souls, and we must repay Him,
but by what price?

Your belief in the One on the cross, is that one token?
Your love of others, is that worth a few more coins?
Your thoughtfulness and love of the spirit
are but some loose change?
Your willingness to serve others unto God,
is that priceless to the Lord?
Will your coins let you enter the house
of the Lord?

Do not let your coins glorify you.
Do not let your thoughts of coins determine your faith.

Only through your faith
can you earn your admission into the Lord's house,
not by coins.

For coins unto Caesar were Caesar's.
That which is due unto God, give to God…

RENDER UNTO GOD

Not coins, but your faith and love for Him.
Faith comes by hearing and believing the love of God.
Faith comes by loving with the heart of Jesus.
Walk by your faith and not by your sight.
Believe in your faith, and believe in the Lord,
it is your repayment to Him.

No coins can ever repay the price the Lord paid for us.
No coins could ever earn your admission
to the Lord's house or to His heart.
Only your faith is worthy to Him.

Render to God the things that are God's.
Repay unto God the things that are due to Him.
Render to Him.
Render your faith and your love.

BEHOLD HIM

Behold Him in the name of Jesus.
Give glory and praise to Him, then commune with the Lord.

Thank You, God, for Your glory, Your love, Your blessings,
which You bestowed upon us.
Thank You, Lord, for this life, Your Son, Jesus Christ,
for the Holy Spirit.

You are almighty God and Lord and to You
we give praise and worship.
We wish to commune with You.
Glory and praise to You; we behold Your name.
The name is Jesus.

Thank You, Lord, for Jesus,
for letting Him come into our lives.
For letting Him live as a man here on earth.
We behold Him only in the highest esteem.
We see Him in everyone around us who
believes in the Lord.
Jesus is present in so many hearts.
Thank You, Lord, for His presence.
We behold Him.

BEHOLD HIM

For unto our eyes You have cast the One
You sent to redeem us.
Thank You for that vision of glory in our presence.
Thank You for the One we now know as King Jesus.

You have given us the One to behold.
Your present of the One to us
is overwhelming in love for our hearts to hold.
Unto us You have sent Him.
We will behold Him all the days of the earth.
We will behold His name.
His name is Jesus, and we will say it reverently on our lips.

We will look upon Him with love
and behold Him with praise.
For He is Your Son, Jesus Christ, the Lamb of God,
and we will behold Him.

MUST BE JESUS

Somebody's knocking…knocking at my door.
Somebody's knocking…calling me for more.
Must be Jesus…must be Jesus.

The door must be opened from within;
there is a key to that lock.
Do you have the key at hand?
The key to the door is your love of Christ.
It is the only way to open the door.
Jesus will not let Himself in;
you must let Him in by opening your door to Him.

Somebody's knocking…knocking at my door.
Somebody's knocking…reaching out for more.
Must be Jesus…must be Jesus.

He is reaching for your heart,
for the truth and the light He has placed within your reach.
Open your heart to the things He has given you.
Use them as one, as the love of Christ,
and let it be your key to open your door to Him.
When you open your door,
you will find more of your love, not just for Him,
but also for others.

He has plans for you.
Open your door to Him;
find what He has asked of you
and wants you to do for Him.
Won't you open your door?

MUST BE JESUS

Searching for your key?
Do not search far; it is there with you.
You had it all the time.
Let your love of Christ turn the lock,
and let Jesus into your heart.
Let your love learn what He has waiting for you.
Let your heart become Christ's heart.

Somebody's knocking…knocking at my door.
Somebody's knocking…calling me for sure.
Must be Jesus…must be Jesus.

It is Jesus, Jesus Christ at your heart's door
Open your door and let Him in.

GUARDIAN STAR

I see the star, but see Him not now.
I see the Light, but see Him not now.
I know it is there, but not right before me.
It is the Star of David. It is our Lord.

It was the Star born to a woman from the seed of God.
It was Jesus, a Light shining undimmed in the night
throughout the world.
It was Jesus, our Guardian Star.

A Light to follow that we see, but don't see now.
He is our Morning Star, our Shelter, our Protector,
our Light, our Guardian Star.

Look beyond your world of worries and woes,
look for your light; you will see Him, but not now.
He will guard and guide you through those days.
The day will come when you will see
your Light of David, but not now.

The men from afar saw the light, the Holy Light,
then followed,
then saw the star, the Guardian Star.
It was Jesus.
As it was for them, it will be for you.
You will see the Star, the Guardian Star,
born of a woman,
a babe just for you, born in night by a Holy Light
sent from the Lord.

GUARDIAN STAR

We will behold Him.
We will see our Star, but not now.
Our Guardian Star will guide us to the right time of His seeing,
but not seen, not now.

Our Guardian Star is there, just believe.
The time of our being with Him, our Guardian Star,
is the time of His being.
The time of His seeing is not ours, not now, not then,
but His when.

Guardian Star, shine to us Your light.
Shine so we may see.
Shine to the time of Your when.

ORNAMENT FOR THE LORD

Free and set apart from others,
different in His spirit and size are you.
Given to you are His laws and His glory,
rich is His love just for you.

You have given your life and trust to the Savior.
He has set you apart from those who have no clue,
no thoughts to His life,
no thoughts of you.

(God Speaking)

You are free and original just as I have created you to be.
You think with your heart and not the heart of others.
You know your life with your original thoughts
and confer not with others.
For I have made you special to My liking and creation.
You are a special ornament for Me,
one that can be hung on My tree of life
in My garden, in My kingdom,
one that can sit on a pedestal in My fields
for Me to gaze on,
one special ornament that is pleasing to My eye.

Original are you, giving of your life to Me,
accepting who you are in My making.
Spun of life through trials and My joy,
an ornament for your Lord.

ORNAMENT FOR THE LORD

Special to Me you have become,
precious in My collection of those in My life.
An ornament for My kingdom,
My kingdom of beauty and special things.
I will have the ornament of your life.

Beautiful is My garden, green and serene,
filled with those who make its beauty.
The garden of My love will be your home.
An ornament showing the character of Christ,
with love and a good heart, one special to Me.

I will hold you up for all to see the goodness of your Lord,
for all to see your life and love of Me,
for all to see, so that they may want to be
an ornament for the Lord.

CHERUBS

They are with us always. They watch us
from afar, but are as close as our shadows.

When we laugh, they laugh. When we talk, they talk.
When we sleep, they need no sleep,
for they rest and stay at watch.

They are our companions from God,
His cherubs, our angels.

They are different from our guardian angels.
The cherubs are there for our feelings and emotions.
When you need to talk, you hear them
whispering to you.
When you need to sleep, they touch your eyes
and you take rest.

When you need to laugh…when you are upset or
depressed…this is the cherub that works the hardest.
This cherub will nudge, tickle, and tease you
to get you to smile or laugh.

For laughter is smiling back at God
for what He has given you.
Your laughter pleases the Lord; you are enjoying
the life He gave, His life.
Smile back at the Lord. It is your way of thanking Him.

CHERUBS

Cherubs, they are God's personal heavenly companions,
created for you.
You have heard you have a guardian angel,
and this is true, but you also have a cherub
whom God has assigned to be right there with you.

They are there when you call out in your emotional times.
When you need release from your distress,
call on them for help to speak, to rest,
but call the most on the one cherub
to make you smile and laugh.

Please God with your laughter, and He will share
your laughter with others.
Your good cheer with His angels is music to Him.
Talk with your cherubs.
God gave you heavenly companions, call on them.
God is pleased and smiling at you, and with
His cherubs you'll be smiling back at God too.

GOD IS GOOD

Look at the sun; look at the sea;
look at the nature that surrounds me.
Look at the animals, the flowers, and shrubs;
look at it all and know of God's love.

God is good, so good to us.
He wants us to enjoy the things He has given to us.
We are not alone on earth, but are all His children,
sharing in the treasures He has placed here
for us to enjoy.

Water to drink, food for our nourishment,
warmth of His sun, and the coolness of His starry nights.
All are glory and treasures given to us by His love.

God is good, so good to us.
He could have given us nothing.
Instead, He gave us love, feelings, emotions,
and His peace to allow our minds to accept others,
accept who we are and who He is.
For He is God and no one comes before Him.

He gave us the warmth of others,
the feeling of their smile deep within us.
The touch of a hand in ours,
the caring and compassion of the heart of Christ
to express His love to others.
Everything He created just for us to feel and enjoy.

GOD IS GOOD

God gave us free will, free will to make decisions
and yet be a part of His life.
It was His way of bestowing on us
His will for His children.

God is good, so good to us.
Our Father is good to His children,
passionate in His life of caring,
open to all who will receive the light of His love.

He has brought us hope,
and His love will show us the way.
He has brought us joy,
for each other to share in His ways.
He has brought us love,
to feel in our hearts and rest in His arms.

God is good, so good to us.
Let us redeem ourselves in His love.

MY DELIGHT

Sent from God with love,
sent to you in a human form,
sent with the angels hovering above,
and given with a mother's love,
He is mine, My Delight.

I sent you Jesus, My Son and life.
I sent you My Love to walk among you as your life.
My precious One given so you may know of Me,
and for you to know of you.
He is Mine, My Delight.

Sent from above, given in love,
grown to a man and taken from life,
all of My doing to show My love,
My love for you and your love for Me.
He is My treasure, My pleasure; pure in My giving, for...
He is Mine, My Delight.

What more could I give,
than to have My son, My life, My love,
be given to you?
What more could I partake
than to share of My love in His life?
What more could you receive
than the gift of My love?
For...He is Mine, My Delight.

MY DELIGHT

I sent Him to share in the treasure of My love.
What better gift to give than My Son, Jesus.
Behold Him.
For...He is Mine, My Delight.

Now make Him yours, your Delight
and know just what you have.
You have the Delight of the love of your Lord.

SPIRIT DIVINE

Spirit divine within my heart,
come find Yourself a home.
Come rest and fill my holy space
and make it as Your own.

Come, Holy Spirit, and fill my heart
as I have invited You to stay with me.
It has been a long time
that you have waited for my asking.
It has been a long time in preparation for
the asking You have waited so patiently to hear.

Long ago, Lord, You knew this day would come,
the day of my asking and understanding for the Spirit
to fill my heart, mind, words, and tongue,
to come to me from You.

Come, Holy Spirit, and guide my way to the Lord.
Guide me from the ways of the flesh
and into the holy ways, so that You will remain
with me forever.

SPIRIT DIVINE

Come as the fire upon me
and enlighten me of the kingdom that awaits.
Let my eyes see and ears hear
what the Lord has waiting for me.
Let me speak with the Spirit upon my tongue.
Let Your Spirit speak the Word of God,
God speaking to the Spirit and then through me.

Come, Holy Spirit, fill my heart.
Make me the way Christ wants me to be.
Come, Spirit, life divine. Come, Holy Spirit, come.

WHISPERS FROM HEAVEN

The sound of music is high notes of excellence.
The melodious sounds are words of God
coming from the lips of his children…His angels.

They are calling His name in praise and worship.
The sounds ring out so sweetly from the angels' voices,
calling out His name in glorious praise and might.
The call is so strong in tone, and yet so soft to the ears
of those who hear it.

If the color of heaven
could have a musical note applied to it,
it would be a high note,
a gentle chord in harmony with the angels' voices.

If the music could have a color applied to it,
it would be one of burnished orange,
sheaves of glitter and gold, blue hues with soft white,
colors eyes have never seen before.

All those colors and musical notes
could not come close to the sound of the voices
whispering from heaven.

Their wings make sounds as soft as air,
but yet are strong in their protection of the Lord.
They are speaking to us, speaking God's Word,
softly as sounds of whispers.

We cannot physically hear the sounds and words,
but we can understand them.
They are felt deep in our hearts and souls,
they are soft as whispers.

Can you hear them?
Turn inward to your soul, your true soul,
the one that is with Christ.
Ask the Lord that you may hear them.
He will answer your plea.
He will open your heart and ears
so that you can hear His music.

The pitches are high, strong, and gentle,
yet soft, ever so soft,
just as the love of God that surrounds you.
You must listen hard, silently, and carefully
not to miss the sounds,
the sounds around Christ.

The notes are light and airy.
His children are singing His name in praise.
Do not miss the music;
it is something never heard before by a human ear,
but softly and sweetly heard by a spiritual ear,
heard by a spiritual heart.

When someone whispers,
you listen hard not to miss the message.
Christ is whispering to you through His angels.
Open your heart to Him, and you will not
miss His message.
You will not miss His music.
You will hear the angels' voices singing,

Glory in the Highest!
Glory in the Highest!

Hear the angels whisper His joyful song.

PRAISE AND WORSHIP

Hallelujah, praise His name. Hallelujah, glorify Him.
Hallelujah, worship Him, for He is God.
No other shall be before Him.

Hallelujah, sing to Him. Hallelujah, give thanks to Him.
Hallelujah, He is almighty. He is everything
and everything is Him.

Always give praise and worship to the Lord.
Do not always go before your Maker
asking for the pleas of your heart.
He knows your pleas.
Please the Lord by calling out His name in praise
and worship; this will please His heart.
Give thanks to the Lord for all He has done in your life,
and thank Him for being in your life.

Do not go looking to the Lord to fill your needs.
Go to the Lord praising His name
and letting Him know how much you love Him,
how much you adore Him and just want to worship Him.
He will love what He hears; it will soften His heart,
and He will give you all the abundance of His heart.

The needs that you have on your heart,
He will provide; just praise Him with your love.
Praise and thank your Creator first, your King;
He will give of His gifts, His love.

Sing out.
Hallelujah, praise His name. Hallelujah, glorify Him.
Hallelujah, worship Him; it is His name, the name of Jesus.

How do you praise and worship the Lord?
Just say and pray,

"Hallelujah, we worship You, Lord.
Hallelujah, we praise You, Lord.
Lord, You are so magnificent in all Your glory.
Hallelujah, we worship and praise You.
We bow before You and uphold You, Lord.

"Thank You for Your Spirit and Your Comforter,
for being in our lives.
Hallelujah, bless us, Lord, with Your love.
Lord, we worship You and appreciate You.
Lord, we worship in spirit and truth.
Lord, we thank You and want to be with You in Your glory.
God, we sing just to You in praise and worship.
Hallelujah, God, we praise and worship Your Holy name."

PERSONAL REFLECTION - PRAISE

❖ When was the last time you praised the Lord?

❖ How do you like to express praise? Praying? Singing? Talking with God?

❖ What are some ways you can reach out to others to praise God?

❖ Why is it important to you to praise the Lord?

❖ Do you praise God in good times and bad times? If not, why?

GRACE

But he said to me, "My grace is sufficient for you, for my power is made perfect in weakness." Therefore I will boast all the more gladly about my weaknesses, so that Christ's power may rest on me.

—2 Corinthians 12:9 (NAB)

THE AGE OF THE BEAUTY

So long ago, but yet so near,
the love of the Lord has not changed,
not changed through time, years, or fears;
it still remains the same.

The endless time seems to go by quickly,
but the love of the Lord remains steady in our lives.
Timeless, priceless, and ageless,
that is the beauty of God's love for all.

Remember the time of the paralytic who could not walk?
God said to him, "Arise and walk,"
and those around could see the beauty of God's work.

The beauty was told in the telling of the prophetic stories,
and how those words were profound;
all heard the beauty of God's Word.

Remember the deliverance of Moses to the children of Israel
for God's promised land?
All saw the beauty of God's wisdom and power.

The Word as it was told of God and His grace,
that Truth and Beauty, has remained timeless and the same.

It will remain timeless through the ages to come,
from your son, to their grandsons.
From the beginning of man,
to his children and his children's children,
through the age of life itself,
the grace and beauty of the Lord remain the same.

The age of the beauty, the beauty of the age;
God's ways, words, and wisdom still remain the same.

BECKONED

I have come to call, to call you in the night,
for you to answer Me with lips of God's love.
I have come to call you home,
home to My Father in heaven,
home to share in My love,
home where peace is forever.

I am calling, calling you to bring others home,
home, for their heartaches to find peace,
home, for their bodies, tired and wanting rest.
I will give you rest and peace.
It will not be in the form as you know it.
It will be as one in Me and My Spirit.
It will be beautiful to you.

I am calling, calling all my shepherds home
to watch over My sheep in the pasture.
So too may I watch over you.
So too may you walk My sheep home.

I am calling you to experience the greatest feeling
of knowing you in Me.
You are chosen for My calling,
My calling to come home, to be with Me in My pastures.
I will give you life and rest.
I have beckoned you—come home.

SORROW

I feel the pain of you inside; I feel the human heart.
For when you ache with pain, I also hurt.

I have felt the pain through the centuries.
The pain of man for what he did.
I have given man grief to experience pain
so man may never forget
the pain My Son endured for you.

I can feel the tears as they fall on your face.
I have heard the crying out at night and day.
Sorrow is felt and comfort must follow.

It is you who has invited Me to feel your pain
by calling My name.
Your voice has not fallen on deaf ears.
You have invited Me, and I will come.
I will give you comfort, for I am always around you
even in your times of sorrow.

I am your comforter in the time of your sorrow,
your healer in the time of your pain.
Never forget Me, for I am here for you to call on
in your time of need.
You will need Me like a child needs a parent
to guide him home and comfort him.

SORROW

I will guide you and soften your pain.
Your sorrows are many; so too were My Son's,
but He found comfort in My name and peace in His soul.
You too will feel the same.

Sorrow is normal to all life,
but a rewarding gift waits for you after the sorrow
has drifted away.

Like the sand that washes on the shore and drifts to sea,
so too will your sorrow drift from you.
It will wash upon you, drift away, and you will be relieved, cleansed,
renewed and rejoiced in the brilliant light of the
Son of God, Jesus Christ.

JEWEL

The beauty of your heart is more precious to Me
than any stone on earth,
more precious than any earthly riches,
more precious to Me than the life I have given you on earth.

Your heart is pure, loving, giving, and caring.
Your heart has always been on others,
and their needs on earth.
Your eyes are meek and mild in My likeness
so others may see Me in you.
Your hands are helping and carrying,
the way I meant your hands to be,
hands to gather the ones along their way
and carry their worries.
So precious to Me is the beauty of your heart,
that your life sparkles in My eyes
like a jewel.

The beauty of your heart seeks for Me and Me for you.
I am here, here for you, My jewel.
You have found Me in the love of your heart.
I have listened and loved your heart forever.
You have never given up your love for Me.
I have seen that love through the years in your heart.
I have seen the peace and love in your eyes,
your ways, and your thoughts of others;
it has not gone unnoticed.

Those who have told the truth about Me
have experienced heartache.
I have shared your heartache through the years.
You have taught of Me and My ways.
You will not be forgotten.
You have been an obedient lamb of Mine.
The path and way I have laid out for you,
you have followed with the love of Me always on your heart.
Never questioning, but just following in the love
of your Lord.

You are precious to Me, and so I shall call you a jewel.
More precious than any stone on earth,
a precious spiritual light in the eyes of your Lord.
You have shared the blessings with others,
and others with many others.
That is the power of My love, and you have obeyed.

Your place beside Me, Jesus Christ, your Lord and God,
will always remain waiting for you.
It will be beautiful. It is like the beauty of a spring day.
Like the beauty of the perfect snowdrop.
Like the beauty of life itself in Me.
So warm and loving, so peaceful and joyous,
so beautiful to you, but so precious to My heart.
Like a brilliant dazzling light of Christ,
like God's jewel.

DAUGHTER OF THE LORD

Friend to many, sister to a few,
mother to some, and now a daughter of the Lord.

I have watched you your entire given life.
I have toiled with you along your way.
I have formed and shaped and reshaped you,
just as a potter with clay, to make you into My vessel,
one which I have wanted you to become from the beginning,
a daughter of the Lord.

I have loved you through all your days.
In days when you did not choose Me
and when you did not go the way I called for you to go,
I still loved you.
You heard My voice, child,
but you turned your ear away.

I have been with you through your dark days,
for you did have dark times,
but you did not see My light, waiting and shining
for you.

Only in the times when you truly called out My name, Jesus,
that cry that I had to place on your heart;
then did you start to hear My voice and obey.

DAUGHTER OF THE LORD

I have always given you an abundance of love,
My love to give to others.
You have done this well to My liking,
but it was not until you truly felt My love
that you knew your pleas and cries for help
had been heard by Me.
Only then did I complete Myself in your life.

You are a kind and loving child of Mine;
I have felt your pain and filled your heart with love,
My love that you now share with others.

The love you shared before was not God's love,
but yours. Now you feel God's true love,
the love of Me in you and you in Me.
That is the love I have wanted you to give to others;
now you obey.

Kind and thoughtful you have always been.
Always traits of My presence, but just never before present to your human eye and heart.

I have been a long time coming;
you knew I was always present in your life,
but you tried to push Me away.
You could not push Me away, child;
I molded you to My liking,
in My likeness, in My character,
My making of a daughter.

I have waited patiently, and you have come.
It is a time of joy and love.
It is a time of happiness not just for you, but for Me.
When one is in Christ with love and joy,
one is complete in Me.
That is My making of a daughter of the Lord.

Daughter of Christ, you are with Me in My love.
Always in My life, always in My love,
always in My heart, and filled always with My spirit.

I will never let you go. I have waited too long for you.
You are now part of My life; I am in you and you in Me.

I have always loved you, daughter;
now My love has finally returned to Me.

PURE AND SIMPLE

Bread of Life so pure and simple.
Body of God divine commune.

Blood of Christ the Word made perfect.
Wine of His wisdom is His truth.

Body and blood His body makes.
His bread and wine we do partake.

Know of His Word and of His feelings.
Not of this earth that we await.

Body of Christ the Word made perfect.
Wine of His wisdom is His truth.

Eat and feel full of the bread most offered.
Drink and feel full of His lasting fruit.

Bread of Life so pure and simple.
Body of God divine commune.

Call us, Lord, to your last table.
Call us, Lord, to be one in You.

MANIFESTATION, THE BREAD OF LIFE

The bread of My body, the blood of My life
give to all My eternal life, life in Me as they take and eat,
life in Me that they have never seen.

The living Word is the Bread of Life,
My life as a form for you to be one in Me.
Feed upon the flesh and know My life.
Feed upon the bread and feel the health of your Lord.

Only when you eat and drink can you know the life
of the spirit of Me.
As you eat of the bread, feel the fulfillment of My Word.
The Word gives you a new life.

The manifestation of My body is for all to see
and remember Me.
The manifestation is quick; I am fast in forming
the presence of Me.

Preparation of your soul in the right place
is needed for My formation, to perform My judgment quickly
on all placed in waiting before Me.

For the body is weak, but the soul is strong.
The body cannot stand in the presence of your Lord,
but your spiritual soul can remain in My presence forever.

You are so hungry for your Lord;
eat of the bread, drink of the blood, and never know
thirst or hunger again.
Eat of the bread, and release the life and love of Me to all.

As you eat, you shall know the difference
between holy and unholy.
You shall know the difference between clean and unclean.
For to enter the house of My Father,
you must come through Me, the Bread of Life.
You must come holy and clean.
You must be prepared to accept Me into your body.

As you join in My feast, you become one in Me.
Eat and know the lasting life in Me.
Join Me in the feast and know the joy.

Become one in Me,
learn all there is to know of the Bread of Life.
Eat the manna from heaven that I am providing to you,
rich from heaven as the body and blood of Me.

Let the blood of salvation and the bread of life overflow,
so others may know the manifestation of the body.
As you eat of the bread, the Bread of Life, you will know
the remembrance of Me.

IF TODAY

Embrace me, God. Do not let me go.
Keep me close to Your heart.
Turn my ears to only Your voice and commands.
Turn me in the direction You want me to go.
Soften my troubled heart.
Harden not my words as they fall upon Your heart.

If today You hear my voice, harden not my words, Lord.
They are words from a troubled heart
going through troubled times.
Please soften the pain.
Give me understanding and wisdom.

(His Response)

If today you hear My voice, harden not your heart.
For today I admonish you who are deceived
by the trickery of your heart.
Remain firm and unshaken in your faith.
You will find rest in your heart.
The rest that can only come through Me,
only if you hear My voice and follow.
You will find all comforts and promises I have made to you.

IF TODAY

Today…today…the time of then and now,
the time to enter into the rest of your Lord,
the time to know of no weariness or pain
or questioning of the heart,
the time to know that you must not fall prey
to a time of disbelief,
like that which fell on the people in the wilderness.

Remember to believe, love, and trust Me.
Through your troubled times
I am here for you to talk with Me.
I am One who has been tempted and tested.
I know your trials. I feel your feelings.
You have belief in One who has been through many times
and knows all, but who, with the love of My Father,
has prevailed.

Today, another day given to you by Me.
Another day promised to you for hearing the voice
who has spoken to you.

If today you hear My voice,
you will not harden your heart,
and you will know your heart
has not hardened Mine.

YOKE OF BURDEN

Take up My staff for Me, He said.
Take up My staff and follow Me.
Take up My staff and lead for Me.
Take up My staff so all may see.

Can you take up My yoke of burden?
Can you carry the load?
Are you ready and are your shoulders strong?
The load is easy, My child. It is not heavy or a burden.
It is light as a dove's wing in flight.
I will not lay heavy My burdens.

To know that you will take it up,
that is pleasing to My heart.
Place My yoke around your neck.
Let it lay on your shoulders.
You will feel the pain of others; you will know
their cries for help.
You will feel their need for love,
their need for My love in their lives.
Share in the burden I carry, and carry the yoke for Me.
You will find it is not a burden,
but a joy, to know My people.

YOKE OF BURDEN

Take up My yoke and you will know
all that I want to reveal to you.
You will know your Lord, your Father.
I will make it known to you, and your eyes will see.
Only to those who take on My yoke will it be revealed.
Only unto their eyes will I reveal their Lord,
for they are the worthy ones of the Lord.

Take up My yoke and follow Me.
Take up My yoke for you to carry.
Take up My yoke and know of Me.
Take up My yoke and your eyes will see.

PAIN… AGONY

The reflection of Christ dying on the cross,
the piercing of His side,
the nails in His hands as He hung on the cross;
that is the pain He felt.
You too shall feel that pain in your heart.

The walking on the cobblestone streets,
the harsh stares of the people,
the hatred that was felt in the air,
the darkness that embraced His people;
That was the agony He endured.
You too shall feel that agony.

(God Speaking)

I felt the pain as I lived in those days and times,
the times when My people lost their way,
and now they are about to lose their souls.
So much pain in their lives.
So much pain now.
You feel the pain; it has not changed.
You feel all the darkness around you.
You know that I am needed now, so much in all lives.

PAIN...AGONY

You are close to Me and know the pain.
You know the uneasiness.
I have revealed this to you to tell others; I am listening.
I feel their pain; I feel your pain.
You have felt Mine; it is the agony of man's sins.

Pain is a remembrance; agony is its partner.
This has been revealed to you.
Tell others so it may be revealed to them.
If they will listen to My voice and look for My light,
they will know pain and agony
is just a remembrance,
not the way chosen to stay or go.

FORGIVE

I forgave you for your sins. Can you forgive others?
Others who have treated you wrong,
others you have committed sins with and against?
Can you forgive?

My Father sent Me as a reminder to man
that sins can be forgiven.
My death was but atonement for you.
My Father took away your sins with My death,
and My Father forgave all.
Can you forgive?

Will you hold hostilities close to your heart
and be filled with thoughts of evil?
Will your heart be contrite and the ugliness
from within show out?
Will you be lost from My calling, because you
cannot hear My voice due to the evil sounds
that fill your ears?
Will you lose and never gain your peace with Me?
Can you forgive?

Only through your admission of sin and
asking for My Father's forgiveness
can you find peace.
Only through your faith and belief
can you feel calm and be at peace with Me.

FORGIVE

The barrier has been removed for you to be
close to Me.
Your sin was the barrier.
I removed that barrier when I was the nail
that was fastened to the cross of life.
I was fastened in a sure place, so you could enter
My kingdom.

I was your atonement for forgiveness.
There are no barriers between you and Me.
Only your unwillingness to forgive has given you discomfort.
You are not at peace.
Learn to forgive.

Forgive all who have hurt and done
or said evil against you.
Then ask Me to come into your heart,
and My Father will hear and come.
You will find your peace and My love.
You will not be as one of them, who were in the crowd,
when I spoke,
"Let one without sin cast the first stone."

You will know, as they did, that the guilt and sorrow
felt in their hearts can only be taken away with the
forgiveness of My Father and My peace.

You must not only forgive, but move on with your Lord.
If you do this, you will feel happiness, serenity,
calmness, and peace.
The feelings you have so longed to feel in your soul,
you will find certainly in Me—in the nail that was fastened
to the cross.
You will feel secure and steady.
Forgive with your heart, feel My grace,
and then be at peace with yourself and with Me.

Can you forgive?
You must; it is the only way to be closer to Me.
Close in peace with your Lord.

LIGHT OF THE WORLD

P

Proceed to the time in your wilderness where you have
looked for the Light.
Pray for that Light to shine the brightness of His life.
Please the Lord by asking Him to shine His light upon you.

A

Ask the Lord to shine His Light upon the path of your life.
Abide in the love the Light will give you.
Accept the Light as your will in your life.

T

Take your love to the Lord at the level He is waiting
for you to achieve.
Teach of the Light; know of its power and strength
as you speak.
Tell of the power of the Light; not just in your life,
but in the world.

H

Help the Lord to Light the world.
Heed His assistance for the dimming of His Light.
Have courage in your faith in the Lord
and walk in the Light of His love.
He is the Light unto your path.

FEAR

It is that which you have called forward.
It is a conditioned emotion...the other is called love.

Fear can capture you and keep you from knowing
the conditions of love, God's love.
Fear keeps the peace of the Lord away from you.

Fear not, for the love of the Lord is around you.
There is no fear in God's love.
Only through full-grown love of God
can you drive out your fears.

What you fear most will come to you.
It will be drawn to you as evil was to Jesus in the desert.
It will overcome you if you let it, but, behold,
you have power over fear, you have the love of the Lord.
God's love is unconditional and ever coming.
It surrounds you; reach out for it.
God knows your every thought and fear.
He searches your heart for your ways.

To thine eyes let your heart be true.
Your ways are searched and altered to the ways of the Lord.
Fear not, for all things are wonderful in the eyes of the Lord,
and fear has no place.

FEAR

The Lord will be with you always and take your fears away.
Thoughts of love in the Lord protect you from your fears.
Love the Lord with all your heart.
Know your fears and be safe,
safe only through the love of the Lord
and to His eyes be true.

THE TREE

The leaves of the tree turn; some blossom, flower, and grow.
So too does your life in Christ, in the eyes of the Lord.
It turns from birth, goes forth with learning,
and grows in the love of the Lord.

The tree gives food for the leaves to grow
just as My Word gives food to your soul.
To know My Word and teachings is to feed from My tree.
To follow and love others is to feed your soul.

My Word spoken to others is like water flowing out
from My branches unto the vines,
feeding, nourishing, providing strength
giving rise to new leaves.
So too I give rise to new souls, like a vine bearing fruit.

I give nourishment to all souls, but yet I say, a leaf that
is cut from the tree and receives no nourishment,
it will wither and die.
So too will souls that do not feed of My feedings;
wither and die
and be lost forever from My sight.

THE TREE

If the tree is not cared for,
the branches will bind and overgrow;
the leaves will lose their nourishment.
So will your soul, if you do not walk, talk,
and live in My ways;
your soul will become as the uncared leaves.
Your soul will wither and die.

You are the fruit of My vine.
Feed on My nourishment; blossom and grow.
You will have Me in your life forever.

HELPLESS HUMAN

I am but a helpless human.
Lord, please come and shadow me.
I need your protection and strength.
I cannot take a step forward unless You will it.
I do not know the way to go unless You show it.
Into your hands I command myself, thoughts,
and my heart.
Walk with me, Lord. Be with me always.
You said the way of the righteous,
the path may be known.

(His Response)

Your weakness causes My strength to grow.
You are not of a helpless heart.
You are strong in My making.
You have given yourself to Me. Your control is My
control. Your thoughts are My thoughts.
Your dependency is My dependency, ever so strong
in the heart of your Lord.
Calling my name and asking Me into your helpless heart
is My making of a strong solider,
always ready to do battle for Me.

HELPLESS HUMAN

You are ready for My coming. You are prepared.
You are strong in Your Lord.
You are not a helpless human except on earth
in your fleshly form.
In your form of My spirit life, one in Me and your Father,
you have My strength.

In weakness, My strength is made perfect.
You are weak…but I am strong.

NOT WORTHY

Lord, I am not worthy for You to enter my heart.
Send forth your Spirit for my soul.
Let Him enter and remain with me.
Speak the Word, and I shall know the way.
I shall know my mission.

I will know I am only worthy
with the covering of Your blood,
the blood that You chose to give me.
The blood that you shed upon the cross for me,
let it cover me and fill me with Your Spirit.

Cover me, Lord, and protect me.
Cover my heart with Your blood,
and let Your Spirit enter my house.
Only with Your Word can this be done.

Choose me, Lord. Choose me as Your servant.
Your servant is ready to serve You.
Here I am, Lord, waiting for You and Your covering.
I cannot enter or go forward without You.
Place me, Lord, in the proper position
for Your hands to lay on me, your child.

Oh, Lord, I am not worthy.
Forgive me for all my vain sins.
I am thankful for my past, one that You
have shown and brought forth to me this day,
a past that I had to endure to come unto You.

NOT WORTHY

Use me, Lord. Use me as Your vessel,
for unto You I give glory.
Shield me, Lord, along the way as I serve,
and allow me to remain with You in Your Kingdom.

I am not worthy, Lord, but by Your covering and grace,
You have made me worthy.
Choose me, Lord…choose me.

THE POTTER'S HAND

You are shaped by the Potter,
molded into My image for Me to love you,
shaped into My likeness, for My glory and praise.

Formed but from dust into a molding so special,
each with the love of your Lord.
Each molding has different specks of life given to it.
Each speck a talent of My giving.
Each speck designed to do My works as I intended.

Why do you think I gave you these special specks?
It is of My doing, given unto you for Me.
The Potter knows your mind and every molding
of your being.
I have loved you along every forming
of your spiritual life.
In your making, I have filled you with My love
and peace.
I have molded you to accept My Word;
take it and know of My moldings.
Unless you take of My Word to know My ways,
you will not be able to please Me, your Potter.

For you were formed of the Potter's hand,
a useful vessel in My making.
So fragile in the making, but unique in design.
Designed by Me for a special use.
You are a vessel for Me.
I will use you for others to come to Me;

that is the gift of your Potter's hand.
Know that you were created for My use.
I have selected you by My choice.
I will use you so others may see the works of My hands.

Just as does a Potter with clay,
I molded you into a character of Christ for Me,
for My using.
I have created you over and over,
molding and remolding until you have become
a unique piece to My eye.

Vessels are created in many ways and forms;
some will give glory; others will show the glory
of their Lord.
Vessels, moldings of clay, specks of dust,
all My doing and choosing,
all for a purpose in My life.

Remolded from dust, remolded in character,
selected by the Potter, renewed in your soul.
Designed for My liking, created by My hands,
that is you from the Potter's mold.

Know of your design and please the Potter's eye.
For as a Potter can choose to break a vessel
and not mend it,
so too can I choose to do with you.

From dust you were formed;
to dust you shall return.
Please your Potter well.

THE SHOES

To put on the shoes of Christ and walk His way
can be hard and difficult.
Some people may mock and laugh
at the one wearing the shoes,
but the Lord will not mock or laugh at you.

The walk can be lonely,
but also one that is always fulfilling with the Lord.
Just as our Father endured the words and ways of others,
so too will the one who places his foot into the shoe.
It is a walk of Christ, a walk of life.

Remember Jesus said, "Take up My cross and follow Me."
It is a decision easy to make, but not easy to do.
To put on the shoes and follow the footsteps of the Lord
is a challenge.
Will you be a follower or a walker of Christ?

One who wears the shoes must speak His Word
and deliver His Word.
The shoes will not fit all, for the shoes are special in size
and deserving only of the Lord.

Painful in fitting, sore to the feet at first,
but comfortable after getting used to the wear;
so too are the ways of Christ as you walk through
the lives of others.

THE SHOES

The shoes will travel to numerous people,
many of them not understanding the meaning of the shoes.
The shoes are meant to tell of the Owner's love for them.

Shoes not made of glass, brass, leather, or wood,
but shoes made of the character of Christ.
Put on the shoes of Christ and walk in His life.
Let the shoes take you to places
the Lord wants you to travel.

Do not be afraid to put on the shoes.
It will be a rewarding journey to walk with the True Owner.
To walk with the One who asked you to wear the shoes
is an impartation of His grace.

Walk His way, talk His way, and follow His way,
the way of the Christ.
Feel His comfort and love in the fit of your shoes.
Your shoes are waiting for you;
put them on.

FOOTSTEPS OF THE RIGHTEOUS

They are ordered by the Lord and placed in order by Him.
Never meant to stay where He does not want them.
It is His will for them to walk
the path they are to go.

(God Speaking)

The walk home is long…the walk to My home.
Walk My journey along the way; learn of My life and of all
I have placed before you.
My angel will not stand in your way as he stood in the way of Balaam
on the way to Moath.
My angel will guide you.
You will not be led astray from the righteous path.
Just as Balaam was not led astray,
never will I do to you.

Follow the path I have prepared for you.
Know that your feet have My strength to walk the path.
Let your feet be as hinds feet on My path.
Sin not against Me, and stay on My righteous path.
The footsteps of the righteous are known only to the man
whom I have touched,
for I make them known only to him.

FOOTSTEPS OF THE RIGHTEOUS

Lean not on your own judgment, but trust in Me.
Your crooked path will be made straight,
and your righteous footsteps, they will walk.
Trust and believe in the faith of your Lord.
My angel will walk with you, not against you.

Walk with Me with your hand in Mine,
and I will lead you down the straightened path.
You will know and understand
that your righteous footsteps are Mine,
ordered to walk as one in Me.

CROSSING OVER

Jesus' love is ever flowing,
like a river running deep.
Walk upon the life of water;
feel His love beneath your feet.

Walk through the precious water He shed just for you.
You will feel the presence of Christ in your life too.
If you will walk upon His water,
your life will be as an ever-flowing river.

(God Speaking)

Walk through the water, cross over to life,
life with Me in My pastures,
pastures and fields green in My making for all
to come and see.
Join in My family, My family of eternal life;
they are waiting for you.

The day will come for you to join them in your time.
Walk across the stream to the other side.
Warm and lovely, green and pure, beautiful and serene,
that is My place for You with Me.

Love will flow like a river;
It will flow through you from Me.
Rest your head upon My shoulder;
I will set all the captives free.
I will give you the rest of your Lord.
It is a place where you can run and not grow weary,
for I am with you.
You will fly in My spirit and rise in the love that
I have given you.

Walk along the banks; look across the water;
see what and who is waiting for you.
One day you will cross the water, and then, My one,
you will truly be one with Me.

SHE IS HOME

She is home
Home in My pastures,
home to share in My eternal kingdom,
home in the house of her Lord.

She has crossed the waters to the other side,
to the land that waits for all I have found worthy
to cross over to Me.
The land is of My green peaceful pastures and love.

Gone are the days of her laughter and cheer.
Gone are the sounds of her voice, her touch,
her fears, and her tears.
Gone are all these things in her human form here on earth,
but not gone from her spiritual form
in My kingdom.

Her laughter, voice, cheer, and touch are here with Me
in her spiritual form in My eternal kingdom,
for these things are needed for My doing
unto others on earth.

Her tears and her fears…there are no tears or
fears in My house, only tears of joy and peace
with the happiness of her Lord.

SHE IS HOME

I have called,—called her home.
Not the way I wanted to call her,
but the way I knew it must be done.
Home with Me to share in My love and to become
one of My angels for those in need.
I will call the young angels home
to help other young ones along their way to Me.
That is she, an angel in My calling.

Pure in faith, innocent at heart, sharing and caring for others,
looking for the good in their hearts;
that is she.
Free in My Spirit, and with the love of her Lord,
she was needed in My calling
for others to see Me in their lives.

I have loved her with an everlasting love.
I have called her, and she is mine.

I have called her;
I have beckoned...and she is home.

THE COMFORTER

There is a comforter in our midst.
One who is among us,
One sent from the Father.
It is His Comforter, His Spirit, the Holy Spirit.
The Father knew we needed One
to comfort us in our loss of Jesus,
so He sent the Holy Spirit to comfort us in love.

In your times of grieving and sorrow,
turn to His Spirit for comfort.
In times of loneliness or despair,
turn to the Comforter for peace.
Turn inward and ask the Lord to provide comfort,
and you will feel the wings of love surround you.
You will feel full of peace and love.
You will feel safe in the arms of your Father,
the Comforter—the Holy Spirit.
You'll feel as if you have given up your will to live,
and you will surrender to His will.

You will fall into the arms of the Lord,
The arms of your Father, the Comforter, the Holy Spirit.
He will carry you and lift you up to a height
only you and the Lord will know,
the highest height in His love with Him.

THE COMFORTER

Pray in his arms,
"Holy Spirit, let Your will be done.
Lift me up and hold me close; provide me comfort, the
comfort of the Lord, the comfort of your love."

In truth and light, you will be free in His Spirit.
Free in the peace of your Comforter.
Free from your grieving, sorrow, loneliness,
fear, and pain.
Free in His arms of love.

He is here! Here for your calling.
If it were not meant to be,
the Lord would not have sent Him.
He is your Comforter.

Do not cry out in anguish; cry out for the Lord,
the Holy Spirit.
He will come; He is here; call Him.

There is a Comforter among us. One in our midst,
One sent from the Father who longs to draw near.
It is the Holy Spirit sent to provide comfort
and calm all our fears.

Sent from the Lord in time for our comfort,
sent with God's love for our tears.

TESTED IN FIRE

Walk in the light of the Spirit.
Rise on the wings of your Lord.
Speak the Word as it is given to you from your Lord,
from the Holy Spirit.
Speak as the tongue of My Spirit to all
so they may understand.
My Spirit is with you always even though I am not;
the Comforter I sent is the Holy Spirit

Follow the way of My Spirit;
ask Him to walk with you, and He will.
Follow in His path, not the path of the flesh.
Your soul is waiting for an opening for the Spirit to enter;
it is there within your heart.
Open the unseen chamber of your heart
for the Spirit to enter and dwell within.
The Spirit will remain as a burning flame in your heart.
The Spirit is the occupant of your soul, and He will remain
as long as the chamber in your heart is open to Him.

Think not with your head, but with your heart.
My Spirit will know how you think.
My Spirit will walk with you if you call.
Walk not after the flesh, but after My Spirit.
The flesh is transparent.
My Spirit will see inside to your heart.
Your character is seen by My Spirit's eye.

TESTED IN FIRE

When your life has been tested to the point of fire upon fire,
then your flesh life will become as gold tested in fire,
pure and to the point of transparency.
You will see My life in you and you in Me.

The purity of your life is reflected in the purity of your faith.
Just as a piece of gold is tested in fire,
so will your faith be tested in trials and sufferings.
Your faith will shine through,
reflecting a Christ-like character in your life.

Your faith is tested in My fire,
accepted by the love of your heart,
transparently seen by your Lord;
that is My purpose for you.

Let your faith reflect the love of your Lord.
Only by your faith and character can your life sustain
the test of fire.
Only with My Spirit can you walk through My fire
and receive the reward that waits for you.

HE AWAITS

The heart beating with rich red blood contains
the cross of life.
The cross…the blood…beating in the heart of Jesus
was the place for the Son of Man.
The Son of Man was laid upon the cross,
but it was God's Son who took man's place on that cross.

The heart was beating vigorously and waiting for the end,
but waiting for He who awaits;
the Holy Spirit

On the cross was the light.
The dove was waiting in the light.
The wings, fluttering with love, hope, and joy
for the One who was coming to take the place
of the Son of Man.

The One who was anxiously waiting
for the heart to stop beating,
to revive the new heart to beat again,
but only possible with Him, the Holy Spirit;
He was waiting.

HE AWAITS

The Holy Spirit was hovering over the Son of Man
to fulfill His duties with man on earth.
The blood was pumping with each breath,
and death was near.
Death was slow in coming,
bringing the blood and beating heart
of Christ to a stop,
man's heart,
but not God's heart.

The Holy Spirit had God's heart
and was waiting to give the new heart
to men of the earth.

The time was near;
the heart stopped, and the light was dim.
It was the physical end of the Son of Man,
but not the end of man.

The wait is over;
the Holy Spirit is here and has come to fulfill
God's duty and plan.
He is with us, the One who waited,
the Holy Spirit.

The blood is beating in a new heart,
a heart of God.

The cross, the heart, the blood—
All were worth giving for His Spirit.

SOMETHING HARMFUL IN YOUR HOUSE

No joy, no love, no happiness or thoughts of the Lord
share a space in your house.
The thoughts you think and dwell on have let you open
the door to a harmful stranger.
The stranger brings darkness, despair, confusion,
and focus on negative emotions to your dwelling.

The one you have let enter in is not the Lord;
it is the enemy.
The enemy in your dwelling will bring you
to think thoughts of you and your problems.
He will stay in your house and wander
from room to room if you let him.

He will keep you in turmoil and taunt you
with his talk that God is not your Savior.
Talk that you need no Savior and can conquer
your problems without the help of the Lord.

The enemy waits until you are at your weakest moment,
and then he will sit down and talk to you.
He will tell you that God is not helping you
and keep you thinking negative thoughts.

Rebuke him; throw that stranger out of your house;
Call out, "Jesus…In the name of Jesus."

SOMETHING HARMFUL IN YOUR HOUSE

The Lord will hear you. He already has,
for He has seen the stranger in your house.
He has waited for you to cast out that stranger.
He has waited for you to call His name, the name of Jesus.

Jesus is with you. He dwells in your house,
but He cannot stay in a house with a harmful stranger.
Just as you would not stay where you were not wanted,
so too will the Lord.

Do not let that stranger in,
for you control the opening of the door to your house.
The stranger will keep you focused on your problems
and not on God as your Savior and as your solution.

The longer you let the stranger stay,
the more comfortable he begins to feel in your house,
the harder it is for you to have him leave.
Your dwelling will become his dwelling.

God gave you a house for His dwelling,
not the gathering place for a harmful stranger.
God wants your dwelling to be His dwelling.
He is your light, your salvation;
He is your Lord.

Focus your thoughts on the Lord.
Fix your house for the Lord to enter and stay with you.
Do not let the stranger in, for he is not a friend of yours,
and you will become a slave of his.

If you feel some uneasiness, feel that something is not right,
feel separated from the Lord,
then go looking in your house for a stranger,
for he is there hiding
in the darkness of your rooms.

Anyone or anything that keeps you separated from the Lord
is harmful to your house.

Clean your house, trust in the Lord.
Open your door not to strangers,
but open the door of your house to the Lord.

THE THIEF

Do not allow the one to rethink your thoughts for you.
Do not be undermined by forsaking thoughts.
Let your thoughts go past the mind into your heart.

Look past the reed that is blowing.
Do not become caught in the wind blowing the reed,
confusing your mind.
Satan is the stirrer of that wind; he is a thief.

Do not let Satan steal your thoughts and dreams.
The Lord has a pocket full of dreams waiting for you,
dreams of hope, love, peace, and joy.
Dreams to make you strong in life
and dreams that will push you past the blowing reed;
past your mind to your heart.

If the reed begins to blow, still it.
Still it with the stronghold of the Lord.
The Lord will guide you to still the blowing reed.
He will guide you to your heart.

Do not become weak.
Weakness blinds the mind and keeps you from going
to your heart.
Do not become confused.
Confusion blinds the mind and keeps you wondering
in the wind that is blowing the reed.

Satan is the creator of confusion.
Do not let that thief take from you what the Lord
has given freely, His loving heart.

The thief will steal time, your thoughts, position,
and anything he can to keep you from thoughts of the Lord.
He will keep you in chaos and confusion.
He will cause distractions and diversions
to keep you from your Lord, your strong holder,
your reed stiller, your strength.

A thief will steal and steal again, freely from those he can.
He will rob from those their glory of the Lord.
Think deep past your mind and go deep to feelings
of your heart.

The thief cannot take the love of the Lord from you.
Your heart contains more riches than
the thief could ever steal, touch, or hold.
The heart of God, he can never handle or touch.

How do you still the blowing reed?
By having the love of God in your heart.
Know of your love of God and you will be able
to avoid the thief.

The thief, Satan, cannot touch you.
Do not lean on your own understanding and
always questioning with the mind.
Do not have a doubting heart,
creating an opening for the thief to enter in,
and keep the reed blowing in the wind.

THE THIEF

Trust the Lord and lean on His wisdom.
Greater is He that is in you, than he that is of the world.

(God Speaking)

I will calm your questioning heart and still the blowing reed.
For I am the Lord, the bearer of the thief taker.
And I am the One who will take the thief away from you,
but only with the love of your heart.

SURRENDER UNTO ME

Pray to Me for surrender. Surrender your life unto Me.
Surrender to Me the life I have asked you to give
unto Me this day.

I ask all that I can get from you in My name.
Give of yourself unto Me,
your whole self to your Father this day.

Surrender your soul unto Me this day.
Speak as I speak to you for others.
It is My will for you to do so.
You are a part of My life, My body, My blood.
Surrender your human form to My spiritual form.
It is My will; you cannot resist; follow My voice.

Give of yourself unto Me.
Your life is not complete without Me.
Surrender the life I have already asked for,
already paid for, already called for.

Say these words:
"Lord Jesus, I surrender myself unto you
from this day forward."

You will then feel the presence of Me
and know that I have accepted your surrendering
from your spiritual tongue.

SURRENDER UNTO ME

Surrender your love to Me.
It will be a day of triumph and completion of My will,
completed on the given day for your soul.

Surrender unto Me, My love,
and become a part of My body; be one in Me.

Surrender your love this day,
and know your importance to Me.
Surrender and you will know the power of My love,
the power of My will.

Surrender unto Me that which is due
and that which I have called forward.

Surrender your life and your love.
Surrender unto Me.

I AM ONE...WE ARE ONE

I am one who is stressed, Lord, and I am in fear.
I am one pulled from side to side.
So many people wanting and needing my time.
So many people looking for more from me.
So many people looking to me for more.
I am one unraveling, Lord, and losing my strength,
my thoughts, patience, and myself in self-pity.
I am one who feels I am in the dark
and not able to find my way out.

I am one who is angry, despondent, lonely, grieving,
tearful, sorrowful, stressed, mad, unhappy, unloved...
a lost-hope person.
I am one suffering from the death of a loved one,
a loved one whom You took from me, Lord.
I am one going through a divorce,
one who has lost all financial gain,
one who is suffering with ailments and pain,
one who feels abandoned by You,
one who is upset,
upset with You, Lord.

I am calling out, "Why? Why, Lord?"
Jesus Christ, please hear my pleading voice and
answer my call, my voice, and my prayers.
Why am I going through this?
Lord, give me Your everlasting gift of peace and
calm this weary soul.

I AM ONE...WE ARE ONE

This is not how I want to be.
Jesus, this not how I want to be with You.
Jesus, help me and let me have Your peace.
Jesus, please hear me!

(His Response)

Be calm; be still; be strong.
There is a change, and you are one who feels it.
The nerves are starting to settle,
and the mind is beginning to clear.
It does not appear as dark; there is light; there is warmth;
there is love; it is My love.
Do not feel lonely or despondent anymore;
feel Me with you.

I am One who knows your pleas and prayers.
I am with you always, but you have not realized it.
I did not abandon you, just as My Father did not
abandon Me.

In your times of trouble,
when it seemed no one listened and cared,
I was there.
When you were mad, angry, and despondent,
I was there.
If you had just turned to Me sooner and called My name,
you would have known,
I was there.

You knew I was there, but it seemed to you I was not.
You are one who forgot your Lord,
but I did not forget you.

You are one who learned that all you had to do
was call My name—Jesus.
You are one who learned it is normal to go through these
troubled times and have these troubled feelings.

For you are just a human whom I have placed
in a troubled world.
You are a human, just as I was,
and I endured troubled times.
So too will you.

Just as you, I did not want to endure My troubled times
when I said, "Father let this cup pass from Me,"
but I chose to endure,
to endure for you, so that you would live a new life in Me.
You will endure so others may see and call on Me.

You are one who knows only I can see all of you,
the whole you, the real you, the good and ugly of you
(for that is what you think, but there is no ugliness in My work),
the happy and sad you,
the you who can praise and snare with your tongue,
the you who cried out to Me in happy times and in anger.
All of you I see and will still love you,
for you are a child of Mine.

In your time of trouble you forgot your source of strength,
and that is the strength of your Lord,
but I never forgot you.

I AM ONE... WE ARE ONE

Pray as you go through these troubled times in your future,
for you will go through them again and again.
Pray that these troubled times will be shortened.
Know of your strength, the strength of your Lord.

Place your trust and strength in Me.
I will get you through these times quickly,
and you will not hurt others with your actions or words.
Others will see and know of your troubled times.
They will call on Me and pray for you.
You will come through quickly
with My hand always with you.

Never forget you are a child of Mine.
Do not forget to ask for My peace,
the peace I give for your asking,
the peace to calm your troubled soul.
Child, never forget the love of your Father.

(response)

Yes, Lord, I am one, as we all are one,
one who will go through troubled times and fears,
one who will not forget you are there for my asking,
for my calling, for me in my troubled times.

I am one, we are one, one child of God.
Let us never forget His love in our pain.

BE CALM...BE STILL

When you need to be one with the Lord,
learn to be calm, be quiet, be still.
Learn to listen for His voice.
Let His words speak to you, and you speak to His Word.
In the presence of the Lord, learn to be reverent.
Be a God-fearing person.

He is in your midst; be still and listen for His commands.
Be quiet, and you will hear the voice you long to hear.
His Spirit will draw near to you, and you will find the life
that you have so long feared.

Be calm, be quiet, and listen for the Lord.
Be humble in your going before the Lord,
giving of yourself to Him.
Be meek and willing unto God when seeking His voice.
Your meekness He will see,
and He will speak His love to you.

Stay in the Lord's Spirit, and you will hear Him.
Be still, and you will know He is God.
In His stillness, you will know this is where you need to be
to experience the power of God.
You will know of your life with the Holy Spirit.
You will know of God's power and His control.
Give Him control, and you will find that place
to be calm, to be still.

A place that you longed to be, a place not hard to earn.
A place that once you get there, you will never
want to leave.
A place to hear His voice and just listen.
He will give you messages of how to bring power to His life,
live in His love, and remain in His peace.

It is God's place of victory.

OH, YE OF LITTLE FAITH

Challenged with time and distresses,
journeying unforeseen to a path unknown,
knowing of the unknown and truth,
that is you—Oh, lost you.

You are of so little faith
that you have not trusted in the Word of the Lord.

The Lord has given you a challenge,
and you have not accepted.
You have let your human ways block His Word and feelings from your heart and ears.
Your own cries you have heard, not those of the Lord.

(God Speaking)

Oh, ye of little faith, have you no trust in your Savior?
Have you no faith in your Lord?
If it had not been so I would not have said it.

Challenged and tested time after time,
but you have not come through with My faith.
Let go to the love of My heart and wondrous ways.
Understand not your ways but Mine,
for I will show you My ways.

OH, YE OF LITTLE FAITH

Oh, ye of little faith, why do I bother?
Why are these times so cumbersome?
Why?
Because I love you,
because you have no faith in Me,
and I must lead you and carry you.
For you are mine and belong to Me.

Test of times, trials of trouble,
come through with the joy and faith of your Lord.
Come through with your faith in Me.
Let go of life, the old life, the way it was and used to be.
Have faith in Me.
Walk with joy and victory through My challenges.

You said you have faith in Me;
now let My trials and tests challenge that faith
and strengthen it.

I AM WITH YOU

I am with you; you are with Me. We are one in My body,
one in My being, just as I have planned.
I created you for My being, and you have finally
become one with Me.
Do not let your soul be troubled if you do not hear Me
at all times.
Do not question my existence within you.

Sometimes will I test your faith and love for Me in My absence.
I will be as a husband who travels from his wife;
does that love leave in a few days? I say not.
I will be as a mother who separates from her children as they grow;
does that love leave and go away? I say not.

So too is My love for you.
I will leave you in times, but never leave you.
My love is always there, just as I am always with you.

You may stray from Me,
but I will never stray from you.
I am your first love and will remain with you all your days.
Keep Me always in your heart; though we may be apart,
we are not.

I AM WITH YOU

You have not heard or felt Me near lately,
but I am near and have heard you.
Never before were you closer to Me than you are now
as you call My name, "Jesus."
The call of my name is the sound I want to hear from you.
At times, I leave so I may hear the voice of one
who is in need of Me.
That is My want, My need, that is love.
My love—Our love.

I am in you and you in Me, always in one heart.
I am with you, never far away.
You are just distant from Me in your longing of My absence.
Feeling distant, you call out, "Jesus!"
and I answer,
"I am here."

JESUS CHRIST, LAMB OF GOD

The day will come in which I shall receive you.
It will be the day of My calling; it will be the day of My judgment;
your judgment in My kingdom,
My body of people.
It will be the day of the Lamb.

I will open my book and call your name.
You'll be judged as others, one no different than the other.
In My book of life, only those
in My calling will be present to hear their names.
All people of the Lord shall be as one,
My One in My calling,
for their names shall be present in My book.

The day of judging I will choose from My book.
Those I covered for My lamb's book,
only those covered will walk forward with Me and in Me
to My kingdom.

All chosen people are a part of My body.
All the people I bless and cover with My blood
will be in the book of the Lamb,
but only My covered ones will be elected.

To be in the book of life is not enough;
to be in the Lamb's book is a choosing.
For I am Jesus Christ, the Lamb of God,
and I will choose for My kingdom
those I find worthy of Me.

JESUS CHRIST, LAMB OF GOD

You are as one, one in My choosing.
I selected and chose you before your making.

My chosen people,
I have put you on earth for a reason,
for each of you to love Me and others,
for all of you are Me.
Come to Me through My love,
become part of My choosing.
Be part of My book, My book of life,
but more importantly,
My Lamb's book.

I have come to save and judge.
Not one different from the other, you are all in My body.
Stand with Me, believe in Me,
My chosen covered people in the Lamb's book.

The book will be opened;
the names will be called only if written in the book.
If your name is not, then I knew you not.
For I have seen wicked ways, and they cannot enter
My kingdom.
All people, not one different from the other, will be judged.
Names cast out; names sent forward; all My doing
in My judging, all in the Lamb's day.

I am the Lamb,
One who was sent among you as your own.
Those who knew of Me and loved Me in their ways
will I call forward from My Lamb's book.
They will reside with Me in My love and be filled
with the treasures of My kingdom.

They will know their Bridegroom, their Protector,
their Savior, their Lily, their Rose of Sharon, their Master,
their God, their Holy Spirit, their Lord, their El Shaddai,
their Messiah, their Yahweh, their Lamb.
They will know all of these are Me, their I AM,
their Lamb of God.

Be with Me in My book, My book of life.
Walk and live with Me in My love
in My Lamb's book.
Let your name be called from My lips.
I will cast My shadow upon you, for I have chosen.

The books were of My making.
All people live, but are not living in My book of life.
All people live, but not living in My Lamb's book.
It is the way I have chosen it to be.
The day of the Lamb will come, and only I will know
the chosen.

All lost, but not lost with My books.
All called, but not called in My books.
Ways not judged, only judgment of the heart by Me.
Live by the book, called by the book.

Let Me not utter, "I do not know you," on the Lamb's day.
Know of yourself and heart.
Know of My books, My ways, and My judgment.
Know of My Spirit and Truth; live in My love.
Love with Me, and live as one of the chosen;
be part of My body as I call the names
on the Lamb's day.

IT IS AS...

Light and breezy wind blowing through the trees,
wind gentle in its sending, soft upon the face,
pleasing to the touch on the body and mind,
wind of the earth, soothing to the body, and
mystically healing to the soul.

It is as...
Rain falling on the leaves of a tree,
dew dripping from the clouds to the ground,
sprinkling water trickling down a window pane,
water misting daily on the face of the sand.

It is as...
The warmth of the sun's rays as they heat up the day,
heat slowly radiating from the sun though a cold body,
a cold lifeless plant birthing to a new life
with the help of the sun.

It is as...
The fluttering of the heart upon hearing, "I love you,"
a smile forming on a face from an emotional happiness,
the lifting of one's spirit upon a compliment received,
following your heart and finding a new one,
falling in love and someone loving you back.

It is...His Word

HE LISTENS

He always listens, even if you think He will not.
He hears you,
He hears your heart, your pleas, your sighs of dismays.
Place the pleas of your heart on His ears;
that is what He wants to hear.

You think you have sinned too much and He will turn away.
You think you are not even worthy to call His name.
You shudder at the thought
of just calling on Him to look at you,
for you feel guilty and ashamed of your sins.
You think, how can God listen or even look at you, a sinner?
But God always listens to the voice of His children.

Do not let your guilt keep you from your Savior.
Do not let anything stand or block your way to the Lord.
He listens—He always listens.

Just talk with Him;
that is all He wants you to do.
Disregard your guilt and feelings.
He will disregard them for you. Can't you?

Confess to your Father your sins and shame.
He will listen, and you will feel a weight lifted from your soul.
Your soul will feel light and airy like an angel
of His kingdom.
Let the Lord take the burden of your shame from you.
He will do this with His listening.

HE LISTENS

Speak out unto the Lord.
Speak of your feelings.
Speak of your heart, He knows all.
He knows what you are going through.

Submit and let go of your admissions.
The Lord will hear.
For the Lord sees all, He knows all, and He is all.
He is the Lord, and He will always listen
to the voice of His child who calls His name.

THE LOVE OF THE LORD

Heart of my heart, the heart of Jesus,
heart of God, the heart of my soul,
love of my life, the love of Jesus,
love of my Lord, who is my control.

(God Speaking)

The treasures of My heart are you and the love
you have for Me.
The treasure of your belief in Me is close to My heart.
My love is always there for you.
You depend on My love forever.
Your love is forever a treasure of Mine.

My love is fulfilling.
My Father's love is overwhelming to you in your human form,
but understandable to you in your spiritual form,
the form that is one with Me in body,
mind, and Spirit.
The form that I want you to be in with Me forever.

THE LOVE OF THE LORD

Find your spiritual form in Me and Mine in you.
For I will see the true you and provide you My love.
It is when you are in this form
that My love is truly felt by you.
It is then that you are the closest to My heart.
It is here you are the true treasure of My love,
the closest to Me, Jesus Christ.
It is here you will feel the love of your Lord.

As you are one in Me, all three,
experience My love for you.
You are My treasure, My true spiritual form,
My one in three.

YOUR COMMISSION

I commission you to speak to others for Me.
You will be a prophesying witness for Me.
I will call upon you to proclaim what you have seen
and let others see it with their eyes.
I commission you to be a witness to speak to others
of the coming of Christ in their lives.

I commission you to proclaim My life as it was,
as it is now, and forever will be
on earth and in My kingdom.
You will be My chariot of fire to tell others on earth
of My love for them and My reigning for their glory.

I commission you to see for others who believe
and have not seen.
It is My will for you to follow and obey the commands
that I have put before you.
It will be through the power of your faith
that all things will be made known to you,
and you will know all things are possible.

You are but asleep if you do not listen and believe.
You are still in the body.
To be awakened without love of Me is but to sleep.
But you have listened and followed the footsteps
like an obedient witness for Me.

YOUR COMMISSION

You are commissioned to be a solider of Mine.
I have commissioned you to serve Me.
This is the duty I have placed before you.
Are you hearing Me?
Yes, soldier of Mine, you have heard. It is your duty.

I will lay My hands upon you
and anoint you with My spirit.
I will lay upon you My commission;
you are ready to serve.

I will give you My power to speak to others for Me.
To go to the sick for Me.
To find the lost sheep for Me.
To ask My angel to lay into your hands My power
to flow through you out to others.
To minister My Word to all who will receive.

I placed certain people with you to minister My love.
Those people are of My placing for My ministry.
You have a ministry with the ones I placed in your path.
Do not stray from them; they are My anointed children.

Ministering for Me is My excellence in My calling.
You are meant to be a disciple of Mine.
You must be disciplined in My Word
to convey My words to others.
I have discipled you...prepared for My anointing.

You are an anointed warrior of Mine,
ready for the spiritual realm of My battles,
ready for the Lord's commission.

A person anointed by My hands, commissioned to go
and teach in the name of the Father,
the Son, and the Holy Spirit,
Commissioned to speak and teach to all
who have been made known to you by Me,
your risen God before you.

Do not doubt what I have placed before your eyes and ears.
Worship Me always, and I will remain with you all the
days of your life.
That is My commission to you; it is now your commission.

I have bestowed this upon you.
Do this in My name, Jesus Christ.

REWARDS

Peace, serenity, happiness, and joy
are your rewards in heaven.

Prayers of glad tidings are ringing out
the praises of the Lord.
Sing out His praise.

You can hear the tones of the angels' voices
as they call upon the earth singing the Lord's praises.
You can hear the Word of the Lord
when He speaks to others through you.
You can see for others when their tears cloud their eyes;
cry out to the Lord to hear their pleas.

(God Speaking)

You are a strong angel on earth
performing My work.
You listen when I call.
You speak when I place the words in you.
You see the needs of others
when I place that need on your heart.

Stay with Me forever in My love.
You are loved not just by Me, but also by My Father.
You will never be forgotten in My paradise of heaven.
I will forget you not.

Your rewards await you:
peace, serenity, happiness, and joy.

PERSONAL REFLECTION - GRACE

❖ Do you feel you are worthy of God's grace? Why?

❖ How has God met your needs with His grace?

❖ God has bestowed grace on you in some way. Do you need to reconcile with someone and extend God's grace? How do you plan to achieve this reconciliation?

❖ Are you receptive to God's voice and plan? His unconditional love for you? What is your attitude towards His grace?

❖ God is a God of grace. How do you interpret God's grace? What do you plan to do with His grace while interacting with others? How will it glorify the Lord?

Write down the vision clearly upon the tablets,
so that one can read it readily.

—Habakkuk 2:2 (NAB)

RECOMMENDED READING

Girzone, Joseph. *Joshua*, Austin, TX: Touchstone Books, 1995

Hall, Mark and Luke, Tim. *LifeStories*, Franklin, TN: Provident Integrity Distribution, 2006

Lucado, Max. *Safe in The Shepherd's Arms*, Nashville, TN: Thomas Nelson, 2002

Mother Teresa, complied by Gonzalez-Balado. *Mother Teresa In My Own Words*, New York, NY: Gramercy, 1996

Meyers, Joyce, *Confident Woman,* Grand Rapids, MI: Hackette Book, 2006

Piper, Don and Murphey, Cecile. *90 Minutes in Heaven*, Grand Rapids, MI: Revell, 2004

Sallee, Marvin and Pope, Candace. *Wheelchair for Sale*, Enumclaw, WA: WinePress, 2007

Simmons, Florence. *Just Common Sense*, Enumclaw, WA: Pleasant Word, 2008

Smith, Alice. *Beyond the Veil*, Ventura, CA: Regal Books, 2003

Stanley, Charles. *Finding Peace*, Nashville, TN: Thomas Nelson, 2003

Waren, Rick. *The Purpose Driven Life*, Grand Rapids, MI: Zondervan, 2002

Wilkinson, Bruce. *Prayer of Jabez*, Sisters, OR: Multnomah Publishers, 2002

Williamns, Jean. *A Little Cream and Sugar*, Enumclaw, WA: Pleasant Word, 2006

Psalm 91

- I will not fear the arrow by day

because You're with me

* establish the works of our hands

CPSIA information can be obtained at www.ICGtesting.com
Printed in the USA
BVOW071404290911

272362BV00002B/2/P